LI̵ ̵
LOVE
LEARN
GROW

A collection of quotes with modern day paradigms for appropriating godly values into our lives and businesses.

Oluwaseun Oyeniran
With Channon Oyeniran

OyESEducation

Oyeniran Education Support – OyES Education, 285 Finch Avenue – Unit 2, Pickering, ON L1V 0E6, Canada

Copyright © 2017 Oluwaseun Oyeniran and Channon Oyeniran
ISBN-13: 978-1981103775
ISBN-10: 1981103775

I love what you've created here. What a cool project! The quotes are inspiring and fresh, they are familiar and yet slightly different. I liked the graphic design, bold, clean, readable and modern. -*Jonathan Puddle*, *publishing Co-Director, Catch The Fire Books, Canada*

The book carries simple but profound truths. It caters to adults and children as well. - **Everod Edwards**, *Pastor, Revivaltime Tabernacle Worldwide Ministries, Canada*

The book is very simple to read and the quotes have touched my life in many ways. - **Olusegun Oyeniran**, *IT Specialist, USA*

I firmly believe that this instrument of wisdom would be an awesome source of encouragement to any reader whether a believer or non-believer. - *Jacqueline Cupid-Woode*, *Founder, Sister Sister, Canada*

We enjoyed the book. In a world that is very hectic and often filled with discouraging news the collection of inspiring quotes coupled with appropriate scripture was uplifting. The format of the book was fitting for a time in history when people feel too busy to spend time in the word. It could be used as a devotion source or just to pick up off the table when needing some encouragement. Thank you for your thoughtfulness. -*Jason Sabourin*, *Officer/Pastor, The Salvation Army, Hope Integrated Ministries, Canada*

This is a very inspiring and uplifting book of quotes. I didn't fully know what to expect when I started to read this book but it exceeded my expectations. With each quote there is a short story/anecdote that ties it together and allow me to relate it to my story. A great purchase. - **Rhysa Luke**, *Book Designer, Canada*

I am very impressed with your knowledge and understanding of the word with applicable valuable quotes as powerful weapons for everyday living. - **Oladele (Dele) Shonowo**, *Financial Analyst, CPA, CMA, Canada*

This is a small but powerful book offering hope and encouragement. It challenges you to be the best you can be. It has some really great quotes for meditation and daily living. I highly recommend it. – **Dr. Ernest Edifor**, *Senior Lecturer, Marketing, Operations And Digital Business, Manchester Metropolitan University, UK*

The Oyenirans have written a gem, full of insightful quotes providing fruitful wisdom to guide reader through the intricacies of life. Including Bible verses, gives the collection of quotes a Biblical foundation, helping people experience its practicality. As an educator myself, I definitely see this as a valuable teaching tool to equip and empower the next generation. - **Daniel Acheampong**, *Primary School Teacher, UK*

These are no meagre quotes, or some daily nuggets; these are words that are sure to transform you, words that are bound to enlighten and strengthen. The Oyenirans have generously shared with us years of rich revelation into God's desires for our generation. Definitely a great purchase! - **Ayodeji Aderibigbe**, *Research Scientist, Purdue University, USA*

The Oyenirans have put together this great piece, the truth in it is deep. It is a good read and the quotes are practical and applicable thoughts to meditate on. -
Oluwadamilotun Popoola, *Pilot In Training, Epic Flight Academy, New Smyrna Beach, Florida USA*

I am not too surprised yet greatly blessed by these gleaning of wisdom put together by my life coach in this book. I

have known the Oyeniran's for years now and several of
the principles in this book I have seen them practice and
teach several persons including myself. Thank you for
taking the bull by the horn and putting these piece both
from God's word and practical life situation into a book. I
know surely that several nations and people will be blessed
as they feed and drink from this fountain of wisdom that
has raised several men including myself - **Temitope
Jacob Awotayo**, *Medical Student, Windsor University School Of
Medicine, St Kitts*

The book is very encouraging and motivating. It is filled
with simple truths. If practiced, it can significantly help all
who partake. Very artistically arranged. - **Sandra Luke**,
Impact Lives Church, Canada.

LIVE. LOVE. LEARN. GROW

As the name will suggest, it is a collection of a number of things. This book is a collection of some of our deep thoughts put together in simple quotes supported with stories, examples and illustration. This book connects the lines between how to:

LIVE - intentionally, positively, purposefully and practically every day and to LOVE - God, yourself and those around you as God loved. This book also captures in a very succinct way a deep desire to LEARN - being aware that every situation, good or bad has something to teach us and to GROW into the fullness of what God has made you to be; the height of your calling.

We present a number of ideas in a succinct way so that each reader will be able to get something tangible and practical. This is not the type of book to just merely read; it is a book that you will need to engage with and take action.

The explanations that follow each quote provides richer context. Each section ends with Reflection Points and Personal Action and Development (PAD) corners to further consolidate the ideas discussed.

From basic solo action items to in-depth practices, the LIVE LOVE LEARN GROW book helps you:

• Rediscover life and get closer to God
• Build deeper intimate relationships
• Develop outstanding interpersonal skills
• Overcome difficult situations
• Love genuinely and wholeheartedly
• Get a clear vision for a purposeful life
• Live a life of significance over and beyond success
• Experience sustainable growth and inspire others
• Strengthen your leadership capabilities

- Embrace diversity and manage conflict effectively
- Turn failure to success
- And more

This book will bless you and re-ignite your passion towards living purposefully, loving yourself and those around you and ultimately taking each experience as a learning opportunity to grow and become a better version of yourself.

Of course, this book is not designed to be a "be-all-end-all" book. Our ultimate desire is to make a justification for everyday ordinary people to imbibe godly Christian values into their daily live endeavours. We believe this will provide a new paradigm for how we see things and contribute to all of us collectively making the world a better place.

This book is dedicated to Araoluwa. That you will appreciate that the most important education in life is not going to happen inside of a formal classroom. We pray that you will live, love, learn and grow into the champion that God has made you to be.

HOW TO READ THIS BOOK

1. Don't just read it. Digest it. Study it. Meditate on it
It is more than just a book of quotes, it contains life
lessons, study scriptures and reflection corners. Highlight
the sections that have exclusive meaning to you. Write on
the margins, circle, asterisk, do anything you feel like
whenever you find words that have particular meaning to
you.

2. Put what you learn to practice. At the end of each line
of thought are reflection questions that will launch you
into your own learning zone leading you to cement and
concretize the learning experience. We have provided
spaces to write your actions points on each section. To
further help you expand and solidify what you learned, we
have provided more free resources at
www.oyeseducation.org/resources.

3. Share within your networks and on social media: quotes,
ideas, contents, etc, anything that jumps out at you as you
study this book. Please include the official social media
handle for this book: Facebook: @livelovelearngrowbook,
Twitter: @livelovelearngr and Instagram:
@livelovelearngrow_ as well as the hashtags
#LiveLoveLearnGrow and #3LG. But don't forget the
copyright policy guiding the book and not share more than
a few lines or paragraphs.

Enjoy!

*While this book stands on Biblical principle, everyone is invited to share in
the learning experience. Even though we know a number of our readers have
been Christians for a longer time, we made effort not to make this book
"over-spiritualized" so that new Christians and everyday people could also
access the truth that we present.*

CONTENTS

LIVE
LOVE
LEARN
GROW

INTRODUCTION
(Please don't skip this ☺)

This book is written for everyday ordinary people who are aspiring for true success and greatness. I am sure it will impact the life of everyone that reads it because it is a very unique book detailing some of the tools, resources, ideas and learning points that has helped me along the way. The journey began right from when I was born and includes challenges, difficulties, failures, successes, triumph and amazing grace I have experienced leading to who I am today. More importantly this book captures who I am becoming as I continue to learn and grow myself.

Born in the early 80s at Ebute Meta/Yaba Local Government Area in Lagos Nigeria, I happen to be the 6th child in the family of 7 children. The 80s was a fascinating point in history. It was a time when the information age was gaining new wings as industrial era gradually gave way. Most of us born at this time will most certainly attest to our dual nature of being technology friendly yet with a fair depth of doing things the old school way. But Nigeria was a really distinct nation at this time in history.

My parents were not that rich. I was not born with any silver or golden spoon. Not that things were terribly bad for my parents, they still managed to buy the Cerelac and SMA baby food we needed. But the 80s was full of many challenges. The then military government ruling Nigeria implemented the Structural Adjustment Programs (SAP) that led to fiscal policy issues and resultant less spending on social infrastructure. This meant that wages grew much slower, household income degenerated and living standards worsened. Inflation sky rocketed. While the nation grappled, little kids of the 80s like myself were left with almost no hope.

Unlike the kinds I see in Canada where I now live with my wife and son, we never had much TV in the 80s in Nigeria due to erratic electricity supply. Those days, we stare at the TV for hours with only the colour bars that is Characteristic of PAL System TV being visible. We finally begin to get signals at 4pm. Viewing starts with the National Anthem on NTA Channel 10. After that we have to start intense prayers in our hearts that we get at least 30minutes of Voltron Cartoon before the electricity get cut off unexpectedly.

The 90s followed with even more interesting tales. I can't tell of how many times in the 90s my Junior high school, Community Grammar School Akowonjo Lagos got flooded and shut down sometimes for months. The *eba*, *efo* (Nigerian meal) and fried fish my mother dished out gracefully in lined up stainless plates every night got us going. Since water never runs in the house, we traveled long distances with buckets on our heads, fetching water for mommy to use to cook.

But my parents never fail to remind us: "if you can put your mind into it, you can become anything you want to become." They strengthened our believe and encouraged us to dream bigger than the current situations that confronted us. They sang to us – *wa dabga, wa joba* (you will grow, you will become a king). They inculcated hardworking spirit, discipline and respect in us and reminded us that God is working in us. Those experiences laid the foundation that I was able to build on over the years. Surviving through those tough times shaped my learning, adaptability and survival process. It also allowed me develop a fundamental skill – mindset. From building toy sports cars from scraps we picked up in the garbage to becoming a graphics designer, a trained economist and a financial investigation expert in a top Canadian Bank, I know so well that if anyone can put their mind to anything in life, believing in themselves, there is nothing they cannot achieve.

It has not been an easy journey but it been a fascinating one. Although my dad put some effort to establishing us on a Christian journey before he passed away in 2001, it was in 2004 while on the university Campus that I became a Christian. That changed the trajectory of my life. I had men and women (some my course mates) who discipled and mentored me and took me through Biblical foundations which I have been able to build on today. So I am not a theologian neither did I attend any seminary at this point. I have only nurtured the truth over the years, listening to great teachers both in the Christian, business, academic and secular circles. I have come to understand that **learning is always happening, information is coded everywhere, but it is only a sensitive mind that can tap into the moment and utilize this for growth.**

As we advance in this information age, building on the Industrial Age 18th-century gains, we have come to a point where the discussion on values is now all important. As GDP per capita gains of the industrial revolution continue to pave way for capitalism we are launched further into today's 21st century Information Age. In this age, characterized by increasing automation, cheap/free access to information, globalization bringing about rapid spread of goods and services, advancement in telecommunication, and so on, we see a need for value orientation to address core foundational pillars that can help us sustain the progress we are making in our societies today.

As we continue to establish our individual identities and create the "You Economy", we see the need to re-imagine, re-create, re-establish and re-enforce the concept of values. It's important we do this because building connected values not only strengthens our structure of community it also creates a sense of identity - a fast depreciating component in our social fabric today. **Value itself being something of worth, nobility and merit; things that are good, classified over and beyond money, with intrinsic benefit that can lead to a higher quality of life.**

And this is what I have captured in this book. Together with my wife who came into the scene in 2010 (got married 2013) and brought a whole wealth of experience in multiculturalization and emancipation she gained over the years through training and practice. Together we continue on this Live, Love, Learn, Grow journey. And we want to invite you to come along with us. We conceptualize these book in three steps which we call the VALUE ADDING LOOP and encourage our readers to adopt. First we present the idea as a value adding proposition. Second, we give the room for you to practice it in your context – practice makes perfect they say. Third, we incorporated a moment of personal reflection where you can allow the learning and growth process to catch up with you (See Appendix 1 for the "Value Adding Loop").

We feel privileged to share some of these thoughts and ideas with you as we look forward to many more great things that will still happen in our life time. Our prayer is that this book will inspire our readers out of obscurity and nothingness to a value state where we can make our world better. We pray it also helps someone to rise up in hope not because of their external environment but because of a change or transformation that will occur in their internal environment and in particular their way of thinking.

Oluwaseun Oyeniran
November 2017

WE INAPPROPRIATELY PLACE GOALS BEFORE GROWTH WHEN IT SHOULD BE THE OTHER WAY. COMMITMENT TO GROWTH CONSISTENTLY ENLARGES OUR CAPABILITY AND ENABLES US TO ACHIEVE NOT ONLY CURRENT GOALS BUT ALSO FUTURE GOALS.

"And the child grew and became strong; he was filled with wisdom, and the grace of God was on him." (Luke 2:40). Note that GROWTH came first.. Jesus ability to grow in spirit and wax stronger prepared Him for the ultimate challenge that was to follow His ministry. Commit to growth, first!

GROWTH NOT JUST GOALS

It sounds funny hearing our generation, the millennials, being referred to as the "microwave" generation. We want it now. Instant this, instant that. We have already started to witness the negative impact of having everything "microwaved". Not a perfect example but it is likely that growing rates of divorce, as an indicator, can be attributed to growing decline in people wanting to take responsibilities for long-term relationships. September 26th 2016 The Telegraph reports: "Brad Pitt and Angelina Jolie's sudden split may well have shocked the Western world, but given how commonplace divorce has become…perhaps it shouldn't have." We also know of many other so-called celebrities who lack integrity and full of numerous personal character flaws. Our kids watch them on TV. Many follow these flawed models and take them as their role models without any careful consideration. We end up with a copycat generation who lack originality and substance.

And not that we don't appreciate logical reasons that warrant divorce, the point is just that we are all caught in the "microwave" syndrome. The fundamental issue is that we pursue after goals instead of learning to grow UP. We totally ignore the process and run after the rewards. **We inappropriately place goals before growth when it should be the other way. It is our commitment to growth that will consistently enlarge our capability and enable us to achieve not only current goals but also future goals.** Growth requires change. Change requires leaving our comfort zone. Growth takes effort and requires careful planning. Goals carry the tendency of achieving them or you fail. Growth considers even the very small incremental improvements even if the final outcome does not lead to goals accomplishments. Note also that growth in this context is not a function of age. It is a matter of the grind, the ability to accept responsibilities.

A perfect example of learning to grow first can be found in Jesus Christ. In Luke 2:40 we read: "And the child grew and became strong; he was filled with wisdom, and the grace of God was on him." GROWTH, his process of being made, came first. Jesus' ability to grow in spirit – spending time studying and asking questions from teachers helped him wax strong ultimately preparing Him for the challenges that was to follow.

Setting goals is great but more than that it is important to grow up. When boys grow up, they develop the spiritual and physical stamina to avoid short-lived relationships and marriages. They will be there [full-time] for their kids through the journey of life [not part-time]. When girls grow up, they become the foundation and pillars of not only a thriving home but also a community that is well nurtured and successful. Growing up in patience, perseverance and long-suffering produces good, strong character. So will you commit to growth and not just goals? Start today by drawing a growth plan not just a goal plan.

Reflection Points:

The last time you set a goal did you factor in the growth component? One of the ways to know whether you had a growth component or only focused on goals is whether you made your outcomes/results a matter of all or nothing. Focusing on only goals is saying you either score 10 or you failed. Growth is saying 7, 5, 2 also counts and if I can score 2 and not return back to zero (a sustainable growth mindset), then I am better off. Growth is the small incremental, measurable improvement we record on a daily basis and not just check mark items on our goals list. Goals inadvertently include growth components but it's only those who actually take time to pause momentarily and measure small improvements that will be able to capture if they are actually growing or only setting goals.

Personal Action and Development:

Review your goals again and check to see if there were certain instances that although you didn't accomplish those goals but recorded improvements no matter how small (see marginal change in Appendix 5). You may fail in reaching your goal but you have richer experience and will do better on your next attempt. Take a moment to record the growth components of your last goal(s) below. What did you find?

A NUMBER OF THINGS CAN BE ACHIEVED AS AN INDIVIDUAL LONE RANGER, BUT MUCH GREATER CAN BE ACHIEVED WHEN WE WORK COLLABORATIVELY. THERE IS POWER IN TEAMWORK.

Ecclesiastes 4:9 says "Two people are better off than one, for they can help each other succeed."

THE POWER OF TEAMWORK

We cannot do everything all by ourselves. We need others to help us. From earth quakes, to social justice issues, to war, poverty, famine, refugee outbreak, ethnic clashes, and so much more, the magnitude of the challenges facing us today presupposes that solutions cannot come from just one person. **When we work with others, building on good relationships, we are able to galvanize our strengths and work in such a way that we build on our collective capabilities to bring about lasting corporate accomplishments or solutions.** Even those that claim the "self-made" title have been helped in one way or the other – by someone else – along their journey. The truth is that one drop of water does not make an ocean.

A lot of us have heard about Apple's co-founder and CEO - Steve Jobs but very few of us have come to realize that Steve Job's greatness was actually connected to the team he worked with. Jobs, a businessman, inventor, and industrial designer had the likes of Steve Wozniak, inventor, electronics engineer, programmer, and technology entrepreneur who worked with him. Wozniak single-handedly developed Apple's first product - Apple I - that launched apple into the mainstream market. Jobs also had a relatively unknown figure to the public, Joanna Hoffman, Apple's international marketing manager to help him. Hoffman played a critical part in Macintosh's early beginnings as the fifth member of its developer team.

Sergey Brin and Larry Page are the co-founders of Google and together, daring the impossible, have probably created the most powerful and accessible information tool of all time – sparking change that swept the world. Brin and Page's relationship was described as follows in *The Google Story* book (by David A. Vise with Mark Malseed): "That combination of dependence on each other, and independence from everyone else, had contributed immeasurably to their astounding success with Google." They depended on each other. Team work!

The Canadian migratory geese demonstrate a good example of the power of teamwork. Every fall, thousands of geese fly from Canada to the southern part of the United States to escape the bitterly cold Canadian winter. As soon as a flock of geese take flight from Canadian waters, they quickly form a V-Shape flying pattern, with one rotating goose in the center lead and all the other geese trailing behind in two close lines. Wildlife scientists have conducted extensive studies to determine why the migratory geese always fly in a distinct V-formation. They found that when geese fly together in V-formation, each goose provides additional lift and reduces air resistance for the goose flying behind it. The v-formation has been estimated to allow flocks fly about 70% farther with the same amount of energy than if each goose flew alone. Geese have discovered that they can reach their destination more quickly and with less energy expended when they fly together in formation.

It's true, we can do some things all by ourselves. But when we work collaboratively as team, we not only do more, we accomplish more. We can spread our effort to reach more people and to yield greater result. Teams working require certain training and skills which can be developed. While each team is unique and may require certain training and skills (which can be developed), we want you to appreciate the power of teamwork. From jointly writing a book to starting a company and partnering with friends to start up a charity, we know so wee how important working together with other people can yield remarkable results. A team working spirit is an essential one.

Reflection Points:
Think about it, the peak of learning and self-evaluation is recognizing where we need help. Certain team working

skills are required to fully harness the power of teamwork. These include openness, communication, respect, participation, sharing, helping, listening, accountability, problem-solving, conflict resolution, etc. You can be a lone ranger and still be ok. But if you want to expand and reach more people or increase your outcomes/output then you need to work together with others.

Personal Action and Development

Are you running a current project that you feel stuck in? Maybe it's time to get some help, open up to others and request that they join you to make a team. Read books that will make you a better team member. List the team skills you can think of (e.g. listening, effective communication, etc) and rank yourself on a sale of 1-10 and see which one you are short of. Develop a plan to improve your team skills either by studying books or meeting with people who can help. We know you will want to know more on this including our top "become a more relatable person list" included in the section titled: "Become More Relatable". We have taken the time to gather resources to help so please head over to the resource on teamwork at www.oyeseducation.org/resources.

CHANGE WILL ALWAYS COME AND IT WILL ALWAYS COST. BUT THE COMMITMENT TO PAY THE PRICE OF POSITIVE CHANGE WILL ULTIMATELY BRING NEW VITALITY AND A FRESH REALITY.

"Forget about what's happened; don't keep going over old history. Be alert, be present. I'm about to do something brand-new. It's bursting out! Don't you see it?" Isaiah 43:19-21 (MSG). Life is all about change. Embrace change. Understand the dynamics of the change confronting you right now and you will realize that it is an opportunity for growth. Keep changing, keep growing.

EMBRACE POSITIVE CHANGE

In David Bayles and Ted Orland's 2001 book, *Art & Fear: Observations on the Perils (and Rewards) of Artmaking*, we read an interesting story on change that occurred in the 1490s. The perspective of everyone in Europe at this time was that the earth was flat. After months of exploration since departure on 3rd August 1492 and losing a ship on the journey, Christopher Columbus returned to Palos, Spain on 15th March 1493 confirming that the earth was indeed round. Right after that moment, almost everyone went back to believing that the earth was flat. Then that generation died, and the next generation grew up believing the world was round. Bayles and Orland concludes: "That is how people change their minds". Truth is, we all resist change. We resist change because we are afraid of the unknown. We resist change because we are afraid of personal loss [security and control]. We resist change because of tradition. We hold the assumption that if something is tradition, it must be better. Note however that because something is traditional doesn't necessarily mean it is better.

Change is not easy and quite honestly, change makes us feel awkward. Change is not always wrong, it just makes us feel different, and that takes us out of our comfort zone. Just like raw diamonds needs to be changed to pure diamond to attain its full value, we also need to embrace change in order to reach our full potentials. To see extra-ordinary results, change is a necessity. As Max De Pree rightly put it, **"We cannot become what we need to be by remaining what we are."** If we truly desire GROWTH, then we must embrace change. In fact, the last time you experienced growth was when you actually left your comfort zone and embraced positive change [take a moment to think about this. Is it true for you as it is for us?]. And change starts from within – in the mind. George Bernard Shaw states, **"Progress is impossible without change; and** those who cannot change their minds cannot change anything"**. More importantly, keep in mind that it is never too late to change.

Change will always come and it will always cost but the commitment to pay the price of positive change will ultimately bring new vitality and a fresh reality. Romans 12:2 (MSG) states: "Don't become so well-adjusted to your culture that you fit into it without even thinking. Instead, fix your attention on God. You'll be changed from the inside out. Readily recognize what he wants from you, and quickly respond to it. Unlike the culture around you, always dragging you down to its level of immaturity, God brings the best out of you, develops well-formed maturity in you."

Reflection Points:
These are the set of questions to ask when the next change situation confronts you. [Benefit-Cost analysis questions]. What real value does sticking with old tradition/old ways of doing things have? Is my refusing to change for the better connected to me not wanting to experience discomfort? [See Appendix 5 on comfort zone versus change). Will this change benefit me or others? Will I gain/benefit more or lose out if I go through this change. Is the timing for this change right? Am I afraid because change will make me look like a student – stripped of my authority and control? Do you agree with us that other than your firm faith and belief in God, every other thing in life should be exposed to positive change?

Personal Action and Development:
Are you ready to embrace positive change today? Start by making a list below of 3 things you will like to see change in your life today. List out the benefit on one side of each and cost on the other side. If the benefit outweighs the

costs, then go right ahead and make those changes. Some changes will come at greater expense. But such change usually come with greater benefits down the line too. Also see Appendix 5 on change process, learning zone, comfort zone and growth zone. Experiencing change is to leave our comfort zone where majority of the people want to be. And although there growth occurs in the learning zone, it could be an unusual experience in the beginning.

Change for good could be daunting causing major discomfort. We are here to encourage you. We are really interested in sharing your change journey with you so use all the various channels to share how you are positively changing and growing with us! Be encouraged on the journey. And can we add a tip here that you share the opening quote on change as you continue. The more you reflect on it, the more you stay the course of change.

THERE IS THE INVISIBLE, THE REALM OF SUPERNATURALITY, WHERE GOD WORKS IN US TO PRODUCE TANGIBLE RESULTS.

"For God is working in you, giving you the desire and the power to do what pleases him." (Philippians 2:13 NLT). Ephesians 3:20 (NLT): Now all glory to God, who is able, through his mighty power at work within us, to accomplish infinitely more than we might ask or think.

TRADING IN THE INVISIBLE

The realm of supernaturality is the spiritual realm where God is working in us, turning our hearts of stone to tender hearts (Ezekiel 36:26). Ephesians 3:20(MSG) says: "God can do anything, you know—far more than you could ever imagine or guess or request in your wildest dreams! He does it not by pushing us around but by working within us, his Spirit deeply and gently within us." Although we cannot see with our physical eyes, the fruits of the spirit that we bear according to Galatians 5:22-23, are manifestations of God's work in our lives. **The realm of supernaturality is the invisible realm of the Holy Spirit. The Holy Spirit bears witness with our spirit that we are sons and daughters of God.**

But the Holy Spirit despite being a deity - omniscient and omnipresent, the third member in the trinity - is also a person. The Holy Spirit knows all things having the ability to guide us into ALL truth (John 16:13) and is everywhere as David exclaimed in Psalm 109:7-8: "Where can I go from Your Spirit?" Yet, being referred to as "Helper", "Teacher", "Comforter" or "Counselor" puts the Holy Spirit to a capacity where characteristics of a person that has intelligence, emotions and will are demonstrated.

It is this divine attributes that allows the Holy Spirit to work in us to produce tangible results. **Trading in the invisible is allowing the person of the Holy Spirit of God permeate our internal and external atmosphere as we trade our mundane qualities to supernatural ones.** Trading in the invisible is what usually occur in the place of solitude (see "Power of solitude" discussed in another section of this book as well as Appendix 3). Trading in the invisible is gaining access to things not yet seen and that are yet to come. When we spend time meditating and reflecting in the presence of the Holy Spirit, God shows us things.

And when God shows us the ultimate, we can surrender our good for God's best.

The realm of the invisible is great! Those of us who are determined to make a significant contribution in our world must learn to trade in the invisible and operate from the realm of supernaturality. Those who operate in the realm of supernaturality not only impact their personal lives and business with a divine touch, fellowshipping with the Holy Spirit ultimately confers on us the knowledge, wisdom and power to perform healing, miracles and other practical things that can be seen. **In short, tangible results follow our ability to trade in the invisible and operate from a realm of supernaturality – where the Holy Spirit dwells.**

So how do we configure our lives to be connected to the realm of supernaturality? First, become a child of God. God has given us (His children) the gift of the Holy Spirit which we receive by faith. Although we can't see or touch this, we have the assurance that it is in us and that God is changing and transforming our lives. Believe.

"Now to Him who is able to [carry out His purpose and] do superabundantly more than all that we dare ask or think [infinitely beyond our greatest prayers, hopes, or dreams], according to His power that is at work within us." Ephesians 3:20 (AMP)

Reflection Points:
Do you believe? Assessing and operating in the realm of supernaturality is real and can happen by faith. God can work in us to bring about his glory. But we need to prepare our spirit. We need to tune in more into our spiritual being, allowing it to be in tune with the Holy Spirit of God. Doing this helps us build our identity from within (see Appendix 7). You are empowered. You can do great things in your life time. Believe. The Holy is at work in you!

Personal Action and Development:

Attempt a study of various scriptures on the nature of the Holy Spirit: Intelligence: John 14:26, Will: 1Corinthians 12:11 and Emotions: Ephesians 4:30. Make effort to be conscious of the effective working of the Holy Spirit in you. As we allow the effective working of the Holy Spirit, ordinary things become extra-ordinary. You can access things unseen and handle them as though they exist. Pray, God help me see into your realm. I want to see your invisible but powerful hand at work in us. See the section on "Power of the Solitude" to learn how to create the atmosphere for the supernatural; where God can minister to you.

UNITY IS THE ART OF BRINGING OUR DIVERSE MINDS AND SKILLSET TO MINDING THE SAME THING; NO IT IS NOT CONFORMITY.

The selection of the twelve disciples shows a diverse bunch with otherwise incompatible assortment of backgrounds (Luke 6:12-16). God was setting up a new structure built on their various backgrounds and origins. When we embrace diversity in the spirit of unity, we give room for everyone to thrive. It is not conforming, it is giving room for new doors of opportunities to open as various individuals contribute their skills and competencies.

EMBRACE UNITY IN DIVERSITY

Unity is the art of bringing our diverse minds and skillset to minding the same thing; no it is not conformity. The selection of the twelve disciples, a diverse bunch, with otherwise incompatible assortment of backgrounds (Luke 6:12-16) shows how intentional God is towards unity in the midst of diversity. Peter - a fishermen by trade, Andrew - a fishermen also, James and his brother John, were sons of Zebedee, a family portrayed in scriptures suggesting they are prominent politically, religiously and economically. Philip appears to be the one in charge of arranging meals and making sure that Jesus and the disciples were fed. Judas, as we know, was in charge of the money. Matthew was a tax collector. And the remaining disciples in the list were of increasing diversity. They were all completely different men with different backgrounds, personalities, temperaments, skills and abilities. They had varying strength and weaknesses which was used to accomplish a common goal. Their selection shows us that God is interested in everyone and can use ordinary people in remarkable ways.

Everyone is valuable and important before God. Even Jesus Christ Himself was the son of a carpenter and was possibly being trained and prepared to take over his father's trade. He never had the profile of who could be regarded as the king of kings. Yet, Jesus is the King of Kings. So we see how God can call and use diverse people irrespective of who they are or what they do.

When we embrace diversity in the spirit of unity, we give room for everyone to thrive. Embracing diversity does not mean we are conforming, it is giving room for new doors of opportunities to open as various individuals contribute their skills and competencies into what we do. Embracing diversity in the spirit of unity creates room to learn values that will serve us on the journey of life. When you love God and his creation, you will also love people around you even though they don't have the same social or cultural background as yourself. **You will love diversity if you love God.**

Embracing diversity enlarges our scope and horizon. It also extends our network into regions of the earth. Embracing unity fosters peace and togetherness. As it has been since the selection of the twelve, diversity continues to be the foundational piece for teams that will thrive in today's world. Businesses need to embrace diversity to unlock new growth frontiers and create room for innovation both in the present and for decades to come. It is not just about meeting workforce diversity numbers or pursuing ethnic product differentiation as some companies do. Businesses diversity models need to evolve consistently embracing, valuing and leveraging diverse skill sets, people and thoughts. Anecdotal evidences show that this helps brand value proposition and bottom-line.

When we are united, the quality of the time and energy we invest in doing things in the community is amplified. Beyond just money donation for community causes, when we embrace the diversity and richness in our community, we develop a loving relationship that causes our focus to shift away from just donations to active participation and engagement.

In demonstrating their unity in heart and mind, first century Christians gave in the diverseness of what they had. Tabitha, a garment maker, made clothes to share with widows in her community (Acts 9:39). Simon, a leatherworker, opens his home to Peter (Acts 10:5). Cornelius, a Roman centurion already known for generosity (Acts 10:4), uses his connections to invite a great number of friends and family to hear the preaching of Peter (Acts 10:24). Others would sell pieces of their possession to help those in need. We have personally come to realize that when we shift our focus from one single source (money) to the richness and diversity of gifts in kind, we truly encourage people to bring their best to the call of service. It is important to keep in mind that diversity creates both strength and values to any group of people or organization that embraces it.

Needless to add that it is upon our unity spots that God has commanded blessings (Psalm 133:1-3). Interacting with diverse people will call for conflict at one point or the other but avoiding unhealthy arguments, having good values, the right attitude and being poised for growth, we will always find a common ground to be receptive of people from backgrounds different from ours. We encourage growth by actually anticipating and involving in other cultures.

Reflection Points:

Let's try out an illustration here. Be honest, how do you feel when you see someone dressed up strangely on the street? What about your reaction the other day you saw someone speak loudly in their mother tongue while they were talking with someone on the phone? Did you think the way we would have thought too? Did you base your judgment on what Nobel Prize winner Daniel Kahneman (author of the book *Thinking, Fast and Slow*) call **heuristics thinking** i.e. thinking based on feeling of likes or dislike?! We were just like you! We look at the dressed up person as a pure stranger, a new immigrant who does not know about our own culture. The loud person on the phone gets a grotesque look too right?.

Ok think about the issue this way now. What if that fellow was born in the same city as ourselves and decided to wear that strange dress as a remembrance of his or her roots. What if the person on the train is just learning how to speak English (hence the loud voice in order to be clear) and probably more advanced in linguistics already knows 2 or 3 different languages while we only know one? Do you see why we need to change our perspectives on diversity? Do you see why we should't jump into conclusion and take the time to embrace the diversity in others? Right?

Personal Action and Development:

Decide from today that you will make conscious efforts not to have prejudicial attitude towards people of different religion, culture or background. Decide that every time you see someone different you will probe to know more. Be deliberate and reasonable in giving positive affirmation as you gracefully encourage diverse people around you. List the top five people you feel are completely different from you and strike a conversation with them. What did you find?

YOU ARE NOT THE ASHES, YOU ARE THE FLAME, A BURNING LIGHT SHINING BRIGHT!

Matthew 5:14 says "You are the light of the world. A city set on a hill cannot be hidden." John in John 5:35 was referred to as "a burning and a shining light". That is a whole new level!

YOU ARE A SHINING AND BURNING LIGHT

In Genesis 1, the "Earth was a soup of nothingness, a bottomless emptiness, an inky blackness. God's Spirit brooded like a bird above the watery abyss. God spoke: "Light!" And light appeared" (verse 1-3 MSG). Here, we saw the purpose of Light. Light was God's answer to end "inky blackness", "soup of nothingness", "bottomless emptiness" and the abysmal situation. The amazing thing is that we have been declared as Light. It sounds really great. But it also means we have to identify ourselves in joint responsibility in doing what God intended Light to do: ending "inky blackness", "soup of nothingness", "bottomless emptiness" and "abysmal situations". We are the Light because our hearts have been renewed when we believe in the only begotten son of the father.

Our spirit man has been renewed and ignited by the Holy Spirit. "For God, who said, "Let light shine out of darkness," made his light shine in our hearts to give us the light of the knowledge of God's glory displayed in the face of Christ." (2 Corinthians 4:6). Jesus, the Life-Light Himself (John 8:12) declared, "You are the Light of The World" (Matthew 5:14). We are here to complete the work of creation, illuminating everywhere with God's grace and glory. We are not the ashes. Ashes indicate past glory – a state of shame, reproach and sorrow (Job 2:8, Job 42:6, 2 Samuel 13:19). It is possible that the struggles of life has killed our flame and passion. Sin could have overridden our joy and zeal. But there is hope today. You can rekindle the zeal of God's Spirit in you by faith. God can visit your heart again and reignite the light. You only have to believe.

Our hearts, passion and love for God must shine through all that we do so that "men will see our good work and return all the glory back to God"

Not only can you shine, you can become a burning, blazing light like it was described of John in John 5:35. The passion of the house of the Lord can consume you (Psalm 69:9) to the point where you become highly flammable to darkness and every form of evil.

Keep in mind that we are not only referring to you blazing as light only in the Church or among believers, we are referring to you making impact in all areas of your life including day-to-day mundane business activities.

This is the level God desires for us to attain. "Not slothful in business; fervent in spirit; serving the Lord" (Romans 12:11 KJV).

Reflection Points:
Do I see myself as a light in my world? If yes, how am I performing my duties of taking "Light" responsibilities (turning soup of nothingness into something of value; turning abysmal situations around for good)? If no, why not? The making of Light is such that our spirit has been regenerated by the Holy Spirit and we live with power, purpose and authority. Our actions, as blazing lights, brings about an effect, an action that reflects God and returns the glory to Him. See more on this topic at oyeseducation.org/resources where you can do a self a self-assessment test on "Diversity of Thought"

Personal Action and Development:
Write below, a list of things the Holy Spirit has laid in your heart that you should do – Light duties?. We believe those things are opportunities to perform "Light" duties. Develop an action plan for them with the power of the Holy Spirit. That is how you shine. Ensure to return the glory to God.

FAILURE IS INDICATIVE OF THE FACT THAT YOU TRIED SOMETHING. DON'T GIVE UP, NEVER QUIT, LEARN FROM THE PROCESS AND TRY AGAIN. YOU WILL SUCCEED.

In the story of the prodigal son in Luke 15:11-32 we see how He left his family and went astray. He later got himself and returned back home. Just like the prodigal son we go through different phases of life and sometimes fail. Yes, we stumble but we can get back up, learn from our mistakes and try again. Prayerfully take your next step and you will succeed.

FAILING FORWARD

The reality of life is that we make mistakes. Sometimes we utterly fail. While not encouraging ignorant, unwise decisions, the fact is that we experience failure when we attempt to do things [usually on first attempt]. Our highest learning since being alive is this: failure is indicative of the fact that you actually tried something. Don't give up, never quit, be persistent, learn from the process and try again. We must learn to "fail forward" by not letting the fear of failure cripple our creativity and passion in life. We must learn to look at failure from a different lens recognizing that not attempting to try in the first case would have been the actual failure. We start here with some examples we gathered over the years and then wrap up with personal experiences.

We stumbled on Richard Branson's profound statement on his Virgin website titled "My letter to 25-year-old me" published on 29 January 2016 in celebration of his 65th birthday. He carefully captured the issue of failure with the following: "The road ahead is pockmarked with many bumps, chasms and forks. There will be times where you want to give up and throw everything in. Don't. By turning challenges into opportunities, you will find success you never realized you were capable of achieving. But you won't always succeed. In fact, you will fail time and time again. That's ok though because failure is an inevitable part of every personal and entrepreneurial journey. It's important to pick yourself up, retrace your steps, look at what went wrong, and learn from your mistakes."

What does Michael Jordan, Henry Ford, KFC's Colonel Harland Sanders and Abraham Lincoln have in common? They know that failure is a stepping stone to success.

Despite being regarded as one of the greatest presidents America ever had, his glum résumé is now generally regarded as "Lincoln Failures List". The list includes loss of job, failed businesses, death of loved one, nervous breakdown, multiple defeat in the run for public office before finally becoming the elected President in 1860.

For Henry Ford, not only did his first invention (the Quadricycle) fail, his first company, Detroit Automotive Company, was disbanded and dissolved. After managing to secure new funding sources, he went ahead to produce another automobile, Model A, which were so flawed with many problems that the Ford Motor Company had to send mechanics to every corner of the country to fix. It would take 5 more years and countless failures before the Ford Motor Company came out with the world's best automobile – the Model T. The Model T revolutionized the automobile industry and brought Ford to the forefront of that industry. Not only that, he eventually helped establish Detroit as one of the biggest, wealthiest cities in America.

Michael Jordan once said: "I have missed more than 9,000 shots in my career. I have lost almost 300 games. On 26 occasions I have been entrusted to take the game-winning shot, and I missed. I have failed over and over and over again in my life. And that is why I succeed."

The story of Kentucky Fried Chicken's Colonel Harland Sanders is truly an inspirational one, demonstrating that irrespective of how many times we have been rejected and no matter our age, we can still achieve great things in life. We only need to persevere and be dedicated. Although there are many versions of Colonel Sanders story, the consistent message we found was that he faced a number of rejections and hardship in life including the demolition of his restaurant. And at age 65 with a car full of cooking supplies, he traveled around making his special fried chicken and eventually opened multiple franchises.

All four of them demonstrated the ability to overcome setbacks, to use failure and the feedback gathered from those failures to fine-tune their approach. Henry Ford concludes: "Failure is simply the opportunity to begin again, this time more intelligently."

This point of not letting failure cripple our progress in life is so important to me (Oluwaseun) because it captures my story. I failed in SS1 (grade 10 equivalent in Canada & USA) and didn't get promoted to SS2. Failing in high school in Nigeria is no joke. You don't get the chance to do summer classes or make up classes like you have it in Canada, UK or USA. You basically have to repeat the class. Yes, you lose a whole year doing both the courses you failed or passed all over again. It was one of the most painful thing that happened to me till date. But it turned out to be a valuable turning point in my life.

I had to let go of my old friends and classmates who got promoted to the next grade while I remained in the class as other junior grades joined me. It was such an embarrassing moment in life. I recalled my dad coming into the school in tears pleading that I was given a chance. They declined his plea, which was the right thing to do. But his tears was what really hit me hard and sank deep into me. I also felt the pain of missing out of my friends and the shame of mingling with new, younger classmates. More importantly, the sheer reproach and stigma against people that failed in class was terrible. So I made up my mind to make the whole pain all worth it. It was a hard process but I developed most of what I am now sharing with you in this book about failure at those painful times in year 2000. Needless to say that I became one of the best in the class upon graduating.

We can count on and on of how failing forward and not fearing to fail can lead to success. From Thomas Edison who as an inventor, made 1,000 unsuccessful attempts at inventing the light bulb to Apple's Steve Jobs, the tech mastermind who dropped out of college, launched Apple company, got kicked out of it and later rejoined when it was failing. Steve Jobs did not only make Apple become an industry leader he transformed the entire consumer computer and phone industry. How about Facebook's Mark Zuckerberg who began as a dorm room-born startup, has so gotten used to failing to the point of now institutionalizing failure at Facebook. The appetite to fail was captured with the initial Facebook motto "Move fast and break things" (the motto has now changed to "Move fast with stable infrastructure"). Speaking on how Facebook has grown to become the world's largest social network, Zuckerberg mentioned in an August 2017 Master of Scale Podcast with Reid Hoffman that approves for thousands of Facebook versions to run simultaneously allowing for many tests to go occur so that failure points can quickly be identified.

Whether it in businesses, relationships or family, and if you choose to call it mistakes, error, defeat, disappointment, malfunction or breakdown, the truth is that we have all had a share of it. Some of us even more so than other. We can't even count how many times we have failed. But through it all, we have learnt to pause, look at the whole process again, see where we missed it, learn from the process and address the situation if we still get the chance or start from the scratch again if we don't. The bottom line is to ensure that we are not holding back or beating ourselves down because of a failed attempt. Through the experiences we have gained, we have become better individuals overall.

In Luke 15:11-32 we saw how the prodigal son left his family and went astray. He later realized his mistake and returned back home. His experience is now richer and broader. He can now manage his father's estate properly because he now has first-hand experience of the economics of survival, wages, income and much more. Just like the prodigal son we go through different phases of life and sometimes fail. Yes, we stumble but we can get back up. The good thing is that there is always a second, and a third and a fourth chance. So own up to your failure, don't argue or deny it. Reflect on the process and seek deeper insight. Review the process again and try again more intelligently. Prayerfully take your next step and you will succeed.

Reflection Points:

Whether it was a small mistake or a mighty failure, one thing was common: they occurred in the process of DOING something. So take a deep breath, pause and then look at the process again. Think about your Strength, Weakness, Opportunities and Threat (SWOT) in view of the process. Work on the weaknesses, access the threats. Don't look outward only. Also look inward. Do you believe you can do it? What do you need to change from within? What external adjustments do you need to make? [I had to keep Nitendo 64 away in order to do my homework and become one of the best in the class I repeated in SS1.] Once you have done all these, try again. Don't be afraid to try again but make sure it's a better shot this time. You will succeed.

Personal Action and Development:

Write down what the weak points that led to the failure were. We call this process "Problem Distillation" - breaking an issue into small atomic units. The "distillation process" may require you accessing your (SWOT) analysis again (see online resource at www.oyeseducation.org for help). The question should be: what do you need to do to make weaknesses become strengths and advantages. Is there a need to build knowledge or ask for help from others? Do you need to take a program, course or find a mentor or support system to help you? It may be that the environment is not supportive enough. Maybe it's an issue of timing.

Whatever it is, distill it down, find the courage to try again. But this time around, more intelligently. Write out your action plan. And even after all is said and done, you still didn't succeed, know that you have succeeded in trying and just somewhere around the corner lies the winning trick.

THE SITUATIONS YOU LIVE IN DON'T HAVE TO LIVE IN YOU, FOR YOU HAVE THE ABILITY TO CREATE A NEW REALITY.

The whole essence of the Bible is to bring hope and to establish a new reality for humanity. Things will continue to happen around us but we must not allow them get into us. Philippians 2:13 says "For it is God which worketh in you both to will and to do of his good pleasure." We can have a new reality.

CREATING NEW REALITIES

The situations we live in could be ugly or unpleasant. Some of us are born and raised in a terribly hostile environment where life expectancy is short and the prospects of breaking out of poverty is significantly low. The fact is that hope is very far to reach in such situation and based on statistics the chances of your survival is very low. But that is not the truth. Facts are not equal to truth. Current situations don't define our destiny. Hard times and unpleasant situations do play some roles but the truth is the ultimate we need to hold unto. **The truth is that a new reality can emerge for you. The truth holds a new reality because it transcends facts and actual current development. Truth launches us in the reality of what we truly are, the original masterpiece that God has made us to be.**

Living in Africa, there was barely electricity and we had to read with rechargeable LED lamps. After a short while of use, they go off due to low batteries. Then we resort to kerosene lamps. Exam times were even tougher as we needed more batteries and kerosene to get us through the long hours of study. On random days when the university activates its back-up electricity which usually lasts for a couple hours. Majority of us line up on the school roads at nights using the street lights to read as the library was already packed full. That was the fact of the day but it didn't remove the faith we had that our future would be better and that we could create new realities for ourselves with the help of God.

Although we grew up in terribly difficult contexts, we saw the bigger picture of where God was taking us. A new reality was born in faith. We allowed God to work in us, to take the test of those horrible experiences and make them a testimony in our future. We were able to endure the hardship and pain because we knew it was a process, it was not an end. **We didn't allow the situations we lived in to zap away our motivation and inspiration. We prayed. We allowed positive affirmation and declarations of faith saturate our minds. It penetrated into our spiritual atmosphere. A new reality came forth. What we did was to allow bad experiences mix in with good responses and that allowed us to learn and grow.**

Another life example we like to share with you is that of someone you probably have heard of: Nick Vujicic. He was born without arms or legs due to an extremely rare tetra-amelia autosomal recessive congenital disorder syndrome caused by gene mutations. His parents did their best to show him love and acceptance despite having many difficulty growing up. Between the ages of eight and ten, Nick struggled to accept his condition and even tried to end his own life. But he later found God. Over time, Nick Vujicic worked on adopting a positive attitude, and, at seventeen, an encounter with his high school janitor inspired him to go into public speaking. Today, Nick's accomplishment is uncountable.

Nick has spoken at the World Economic Forum in Davos, spoken to six presidents, and over 50 million people have seen him in action on the internet. His memoir, Love Without Limits has now been published in multiple languages. Nick has accomplished more than most people achieve in a lifetime. He's an author, musician and actor. Vujicic runs a non-profit ministry, Life Without Limbs, as well as Attitude is Altitude, which markets his motivational speeches and campaigns against bullying.

Nick concludes: 'Brokenness can be a good thing'. He further added during his 2015 TV debut on TLC: "I need the wings of the Holy Spirit," he said. "I'm flying, because I know Jesus is holding me up." **Nick's life shows how we**

can learn to accept what we cannot control and focus instead on what we can. Our belief, even our faith.

Today, these experiences create the opportunity to share with you that no matter what circumstances you are in, you can create a new reality. **It requires the exercise of faith. Remove yourself from the limbo. Be in an environment of people who see and believe a new reality.** God said in Isaiah 43:19, "Behold, I will do a new thing; now it shall spring forth; shall ye not know it? I will even make a way in the wilderness, and rivers in the desert." "Therefore, if anyone is in Christ, he is a new creation; old things have passed away; behold, all things have become new." — 2 Corinthians 5:17. "See, I will create new heavens and a new earth. The former things will not be remembered, nor will they come to mind." — Isaiah 65:17. Believe God's word, a new reality is already emerging for you.

Reflection Points:
What does your situation look like? Not-so-good? Fair? Good? Whatever your answer is, it can still be better. For some, it may be so terrible you don't even want to talk about it. We understand with you. We just want you to reflect on the truth which is this: what you see now is just temporary. This too will pass away. What is important is your faith and what you see ahead. A glorious destiny? Yes. Can you envision a new reality? Meditate on the big picture God has shown you of a bright future – here on earth and not only in heaven. Let it strengthen you through the journey as you continue to meditate on God's word – it will shift your atmosphere for good. **God can cause heaven to be open for you as you submit to the truth in His word.**

Personal Action and Development:
Write out the new reality you want to see. Write out the names of those who are in a similar context with you and desire a similar new reality. Practice solitude moments often

and get a clear vision (see other section on the power of solitude as well as the section on vision). This was exactly how I made it through those tough times. I had a picture on my wall of what I was trusting God for. I was in the midst of godly people. We shared the word of God together. So get a list of scriptures and words to fire you up through the journey so you don't get discouraged or demoralized. Keep walking and working towards a new reality. Believe.

YOU DON'T HAVE A SAY AS PER WHERE YOU ARE BORN, BUT YOU HAVE THE POWER TO CHOOSE NOT TO LET THIS AFFECT YOU NEGATIVELY.

The good thing is that although we didn't have a say in the beginning of the stories of our lives, we have the ability to receive God's enabling power and grace to make choices that will make the concluding chapters a remarkable one. The choice is ours. Deuteronomy 30:15 says "Now listen! Today I am giving you a choice between life and death, between prosperity and disaster."

YOU CAN CHOOSE TO CHANGE YOUR STORY

Some live sad lives: complaining about who their parents are or why they belong to a specific family, culture or country. If such people had the chance to choose their birth place they would probably choose a totally different location. Unfortunately we don't have a say as per where, when, how or to whom we were born. **The important thing for you to note here however is this: your birth is not a mistake.** You were pre-designed with a purpose and God preconceived you in His mind long before you were born. Yes, God has a mind because He can think (God's thought: Jeremiah 29:11).

William Manchester once wrote a biography of Winston Churchill in the book *Winston Spencer Churchill: The Last Lion, Visions of Glory*. William included this short story in the book talking about Churchill: "Sickly, an uncoordinated weakling with the pale fragile hands of a girl, speaking with a lisp and a slight stutter, he had been at the mercy of bullies. They beat him, ridiculed him, and pelted him with cricket balls. Trembling and humiliated, he hid in a nearby woods. This was hardly the stuff of which gladiators are made." Winston Churchill grew to become a "gladiator", leading the charge against Adolf Hitler as Britain's Prime Minister during the Second World War. Winston Churchill has been viewed as one of the shinning lights of the 20th century ever since then. In fact, *Spiegel Online* (a popular European international online news agency) dubbed Winston Churchill as "The man who saved Europe" Winston Churchill chose to change his story for good.

As discussed in the previous section, we must not allow the situations we live in to live inside of us. **We must choose to make our stories end well irrespective of where, how or when we were born.**

Your life is not an arbitrary one. It's all for a purpose. **Where you were born, where you would live, your race, nationality and other cultural identity are not accidents. They were amazingly decided by God with great precision.** Regardless of the circumstances of your birth or who your parents are, God has a plan in creating you. It doesn't matter whether your parents were good, bad, or indifferent. God knew that those two individuals possessed exactly the right genetic makeup to create the custom 'you' He had in mind. They had the DNA God wanted to use to form you. **While there are illegitimate parents, there are no illegitimate children.** Many children are unplanned by their parents, but they are not unplanned by God. **God's purpose took into account human error and even sin.** So don't hold your parent or anyone else accountable for your ordeal in life. Take charge, take responsibility. Understand that God is putting the puzzle of your life together. Agree with God. Believe His report for you.

In Ephesians 1:4a (MSG) we find a great report: "Long before he laid down earth's foundations, he had us in mind, had settled on us as the focus of his love, to be made whole and holy by his love." In Jeremiah 1:5 (NKJV) it is written: "Before I formed you in the womb I knew you; Before you were born I sanctified you; I ordained you a prophet to the nations." God decided to give us life through the word of truth so we might be the most important of all the things he made (James 1:18 NCV). This is how much God loves and values you!

Life experiences could be critical but more importantly, our responses to them can be critically more important. We have the power to choose to respond positively. Your response has to be based on believing that God had you in mind from the onset. The Holy Spirit has been made available to you when you believed in the only begotten son of God, Jesus Christ. With the Holy Spirit in you, you have the power to set the course of your destiny as you begin to see with the eyes of faith.

As we wrap up this section, we must not fail to mention how important your voice can be in shaping your choice. We must not underestimate how powerful our word can be. Learn to make positive declarations upon yourself. Our words, what we constantly say to ourselves, have effects on our brains. Words become flesh. Words inadvertently become life. And as vital as our words can be in shaping our choices and destinies, it is free! So declare God's word towards yourself today. Decree, prophesy, declare. Be deliberate about it. Choose to speak greatness into your life.

Life is all about choices. You can either choose to play victim, or accept God's report that you were born of Him and that you have a purpose and destiny in Him. God knew us from the very beginning and has made us "predestined to be conformed to the image of his Son" (Romans 8:29). Choose to believe God's report.

Reflection Points:

What has your experiences been when you think of where you were born? [Country, Home, Family, Lineage]? How have you responded? Does your response need to change? Do you believe God's report for your life? Appreciate that nothing is a mistake before God. Take a moment to think about this carefully: your parents don't have the final say, God does. So choose to see through what he created – you – the original. Chances are that there is something really special in store for you.

Personal Action and Development:

Go through some of the scriptures above again. This time more carefully. Write them out somewhere and meditate on them frequently. Memorize them. Do that for a couple days and see how it is changing your perception about the purpose of your life in the context of where you were born.

IN THE SCHOOL OF EFFECTIVE GROWTH, IMPROVEMENT AND CHANGE GO HAND IN HAND. TO ENTER THE NEW IS TO BREAK FROM COMFORT.

Brothers and sisters, I do not consider myself yet to have taken hold of it. But one thing I do: Forgetting what is behind and straining toward what is ahead, I press on toward the goal to win the prize for which God has called me heavenward in Christ Jesus" – Philippians 3: 13-14 (NIV)

BREAKING LOOSE FROM YOUR INERTIA

Continuous improvement is a term many of us who work for large corporation have become familiar with. Continuous improvements are built on strong internal change culture in these corporations. Not only do firms implement improvement framework to meet regulatory requirements, continuous improvement helps in mitigating risks. And because risks are constantly and rapidly changing, risk mitigating measures and controls have to continue to change as well. Leading companies tend to be growth oriented as they maintain internal agility that allows them to quickly break from comfortable, high-risk state to an evolving and continuously compliant state. **Just like growth-oriented corporations, we too, in order to be compliant and able to mitigate coming risk that society or life will inflict on us, have to keep changing and improving on ourselves. Continuous change and improvement bring about effective growth.**

Our comfort zone is where we are safe. Comfort zones limit our dreams, potentials and encourages mediocrity. Things are easy and predictable and we spend most of our time in the comfort zone (see Appendix 5 for the comfort zone versus learning zone diagram). Our comfort zone is like a state of rest, an inertia, where there is no change in momentum. Staying in the comfort zone is like going to the gym every day and doing the same exercises for months and months. There would be no significant change or improvement. Coming out of our comfort zone is to enter the new, the learning zone. This is where you push the boundaries of your existing skills and experience. This is where real learning and growth takes place.

Daniel H. Pink put it well in his book *Drive: The Surprising Truth About What Motivates Us*, with the following:

"We need a place of productive discomfort, if you're too comfortable, you're not productive. And if you're too uncomfortable, you're not productive. Like Goldilocks [and the bears], we can't be too hot or too cold."

If you've ever pushed yourself to get to the next level in sports, fitness or by learning a new skill, you know what it's like to step outside your comfort zone. You know what it's like in the learning zone. **To transition away into being a novice can be tough. Breaking from our comfort zone and entering the new can be a truly daunting process. Yet it is the most rewarding. Growth can be exhilarating yet painful, gainful yet uncomfortable.** However, once the leap is taken, often the development is valuable and adds to the richness of our experience. Disrupting ourselves can truly open up a world of opportunities.

We would like to share the following process we tried ourselves and recommend for you. First, recognize that remaining in your comfort zone will create negative impacts on your ability to live purposefully and to reach your full potential. Second, do a personal audit and identify areas that you can make small, marginal adjustments that will expose you to new experiences. Experiences that will challenge you to grow. Small adjustments may include adding more distances to the jogging routine or treadmill or leaving work early to cook dinner or changing your relationships or social circles.

Second, you will then need to assess your environment and social networks. It is ideal to break from relationships that are not helping you grow and focusing on the ones that will strengthen your resolve to get better (See "Relationship Tenet" in Appendix 4). Third, set small achievable growth objectives – little incremental measurable change – steps that can be sustained over time. Finally, like Jesus Christ in

Philippians 2, who focused on the destination and not the agony of the present moment, set your minds to something greater. Aim to become a better, more responsible and empowered individual. In the end, we trust that you will reap all the benefits of the effective growth process.

Reflection Points:

Think about this carefully, is it true that the last time you experienced growth was when you exited your comfort zone and extended your usual physical or mental borders/limits? Are you aspiring to become a better leader? Note that leadership develops in your learning zone. Are you willing to feel awkward and uncomfortable in order to gain improvement and growth? Think clear: effective growth requires moving from comfort zone to the learning zone and learning zone makes you a student once again. Can you imagine what being a student will be like again? Being instructed, tossed around and told what to do and when homeworks are due? But therein lies the opportunity for growth. Right? So when last did you try something new?

Personal Action and Development:

Try something new. If positive change is not imposed on you by an external factor (say a leader, trainer or a mentor), make effort to impose it on yourself. Change the routine of whatever it is you intend to experience growth in. Take a moment to review Appendix 5. Add a little more weight in the gym, walk longer distances, raise the bar to the next level. You can do it. You may combine this with other action items listed in other sections of this book e.g. traveling. Breaking from comfort may actually mean for a senior executive to decide to join the operation department as an ordinary staff for a couple days to see what new learning zone opportunity will accrue. One can decide to find new acquaintances from a different background. And so on. The aim is to initiate a change process into the learning zone. Write out what you learned from these new experience if you eventually tried it out. Could you note any new skills developed?

OUR FOCUS SHOULD NOT BE TO OUT-COMPETE OTHERS. THE FOCUS SHOULD BE TO BECOME A BETTER VERSION OF OURSELVES WITH EACH PASSING DAY; GOING A STEP FURTHER AND BEING TRANSFORMED FROM GLORY TO GLORY.

Oh, don't worry; we wouldn't dare say that we are as wonderful as these other men who tell you how important they are! But they are only comparing themselves with each other, using themselves as the standard of measurement. How ignorant! - 2 Corinthians 10:12 (NLT)

YOU HAVE A DIVINE PATHWAY – AVOID COPYING AND UNHEALTHY COMPETITION

God is the designer and architect of every life and has pre-ordained a peculiar life route for each one of us. The road to our destination is really not a straight path as we often assume. It is wobbly, filled with many ups and downs, valleys and mountains, high moments and low moments. If we don't lose connection and communication with the author and designer of our lives we will hold steady through the highs and the lows and ultimately come out golden. Somehow, sadly, we have been made to believe that the journey to "arrive" at our destination is a straight, easy road. More disheartening is that we spend a huge part of our lives "copying" or "competing" with others who sometimes are on their own divine route. We easily get deceived by the appearance of those who "act" like they have "arrived" when in most cases they are on a totally wrong pathway. Why copy or compete when, out of the 7.2 billion people on earth, you are a Divine Original? **Sometimes we copy people that have "made it" under the guise of mentorship.**

There are now many mentors, some unofficial, from YouTube tutorials to business blogs and other platforms. Sometimes we look for celebrities who have no credibility in mentorship to become our mentors. We have nothing against mentorship because true mentors have the ability to guide and open our minds to new possibilities we never saw in ourselves. Positive role models and mentors are good to the extent that they lead us to our own divine pathway. But we have come across a lot of mentorship in recent times where both the mentee and the mentor don't have a clear grasp of the mentorship process. It is when mentorship takes people out of their divine pathways, becomes a selfish process and does not lead to growth that it raises concerns. We recently read of a mentorship experience where a potential mentee in the process of searching for a mentor made a list of request including payment for services offered and other terms and conditions the mentor needs to fulfil.

We need to therefore approach mentorship with caution as it could lead to mindlessly copying our so called "mentors" when it should actually be to discover ourselves and unravel our own full potentials. **Mentees should go to mentorship with something to offer as well; not only to take. Mentors should see mentorship opportunities as a privilege to guide, nurture and elevate our mentees along their divine pathways.**

The issue is that copying (anyone including our mentors) or competing (especially against our pairs) produces little or no new ideas. 2 Corinthians 10:12 concludes that it demonstrates lack of wisdom. So this is it: our focus should not be to out-compete others. While healthy competition could have some benefit, the focus should be to become a better version of ourselves with each passing day; going a step further on our unique pathway and striving for the best we can be. Competition creates a win or lose mindset which could sometimes be unhealthy. Yes, we miss it sometimes, copying (stealing) someone else's model or aggressively competing wrongly. There is room to return back to our own divine pathway today – right now.

Where do you start from you ask? First: seek to know the designer - God. Second, pray for a revelation of the blueprint - the map for the journey. Third: follow your unique pathway. Receive fresh instruction and inspiration for navigating through your Divine Pathway today. We described this process of living out/establishing your identity from the core of who God has made you in Appendix 7.

Life is a journey, not a competition. We must train our minds to celebrate success and be happy irrespective of whether it pertains to our friends or foe. You will find more inspiration to be the divine original that God has made you to be as you continue on your divine pathway. God will show you men and women (mentors) who you can contribute to their learning experience and develop a mentorship relationship with. Part of our objective with this book is to help our readers to assess their mentorship relationship and to feel fresh and original as they tap into the core of their identity and being. **Mentorship can help but above all, we encourage you today, strive to be a better version of yourself.**

Reflection Points:

We know, our world thrives on competition. But come to think of it, to what extent do we compete? And what if instead of copying we set our minds on building the new? What if we focus on getting better in our craft by tapping from a creativity source that is out of this world, God. What about reviewing our approach to mentorship? Are we intending mentorship to be for copying or contributing, demand or develop, to give or to take? We found good mentorship requires both ends giving. Do you agree or find this to be true also?

Personal Action and Development:

It will take some real effort but take a look at yourself and identify the few areas you feel you flourish. Look again and list out what has worked and what has not worked. Things that worked and you flourished in are pointers to your divine pathway. Expand on what has worked and prayerfully ask God to give you fresh inspiration and ideas to set the bar higher in your industry, career or business. Your better version, the original you, is your unique advantage. Make it your watchword not to compete but to develop yourself through effecting learning and practice.

TO MAKE CERTAIN THAT THE BLOOD, SWEAT AND TEARS OF THOSE THAT WENT AHEAD OF US DID NOT GO IN VAIN, WE NEED TO LOOK AND LEARN FROM THE PAST TO MAKE OUR TODAY AND FUTURE DIFFERENT, BETTER AND HOPEFUL. THEIR FAITH IS OUR SHINING SHIELD.

The faith of those who went before us sowed the seed for us today. We owe it to them to fulfill the call, promise and destiny that God has for us His children. We will take up where their faith left off and allow our faith and hope to complete the purpose God has for us. In Hebrews 11:39-40 we can clearly see that the heroes of faith are awaiting our exploits.

HEROES OF FAITH AND THE GREAT CLOUD OF WITNESS

Hebrews 11 shows us the account of great men and women of old who through their exploits of faith paved the foundation for Christianity today. They went through a lot. Moses could have had treasures and pleasures of Egypt, but he chose to give it all up to serve God and suffer in wilderness. Through trials and temptations, they prevailed. Like John H. Yates (1891) puts it in the song, *Faith Is The Victory*, "The faith by which THEY conquered death Is still OUR shining shield." While there are those of Biblical times, we also have men and women who centuries and decades ago have worked hard in the fight for freedom, justice equality and other human rights. Historical figures, some of who lost their lives in the battle. They still minister to us today.

The battle continues into our present day. The challenges we face today presupposes that we need the very same virtue that was at work in these great men and women. We are not just wrestling against flesh and blood (Ephesians 6:12-13) so our weapon of warfare cannot be the same as that which is being used against us. We need something more. **When we fight in the realm of faith as these men and women of old did, God arises and fights for us. That is the realm we need to operate in, as we uphold the principles of non-violence; knowing fully well that the prayer room is our war room.**

Today, these heroes of faith stand cheering us on like a great cloud of witness (Hebrews 12:1). They have gone on before us, already lived their lives, suffered for their faith, and remained faithful. They are now our encouragers. They are telling us that it will not be easy, but if they could do it, we can do it too. They are reminding us that our ultimate triumph in life determines their own victory as well. Yes, "we are surrounded by so great a cloud of witnesses."

As we continue to tread on their pathways of faith, we create the exploits of today, bringing down God's glory in our respective endeavors. Through faith, we too can, just as they have done, change the course of history. We can create an environment of spiritual, material, and economic growth by exploring the self-same pathway of faith they present to us. Their effort must not go in vain. We can look and learn from the past to make our today and future different, better and hopeful. Truly, our ultimate reward is in heaven. There is a prize that is greater than what we can see here on earth.

Reflection Points:

Whether in your family line or not, there are certain people that comes to mind when we think of heroes of faith. Men and women who have worked hard and laboured to set a good path for us to follow. They cut across many sectors, a large number of which are not even known publicly. Take a moment to think about them; their works and legacy. Look back and learn from them.

Personal Action and Development:

List out a few heroes of faith that comes to your mind below. Although we recommend people who are of recent (in our family or in our own history books) but Biblical heroes of faith suffice too. In front of each of their names, put the life lessons and examples they have set for you. Is there any of them that is closer to you who you have received gifts or have their souvenirs? Bring those souvenirs out today. Not out of pity or sadness, but as a reflection of the strong legacy and impact they have made not only to you but others as well. Celebrate them and live to continue their legacy.

WHETHER ITS PEOPLE OR INDIVIDUAL CONCERNS, PROBLEMS WITH PROCESS OR OPERATIONS, GOOD LEADERSHIP CURES EVERYTHING.

Jesus Christ is the symbol of great leadership. He is humble enough to serve others, washing their feet and meeting them at the very point of their needs (John 13:12-15). Yet in terms of kingdom business, he was the master; silencing the devil (Mat 4:10, Luke 4:8), putting demons and principalities in their place (Luke 11:14, Mark 1:34, 39) and completing the redemption operation with power and grace (John 17:4). Even at the very point of his death on the cross, His outstanding servant leadership was made manifest (Phil 2:8).

GOOD LEADERSHIP CURES MANY THINGS

Leadership is so crucial. It can cure many things. John C. Maxwell was right: "Everything rises and falls on leadership". In the course of our lives, we have seen various leadership paradigms: Autocratic, laissez-faire, democratic, situational, etc. Of all the leadership styles, we found servant leadership to be the most unique and probably most accurate to attend to most of today's need for leadership.

Servant leadership is good leadership. Our definition of servant leadership is when a leader places the needs of others first with the intent of meeting these needs, equipping them and empowering them to in turn do the same for others. We found this very well captured in the leadership style of Jesus Christ. With concerns of individuals and people constantly increasing as we deal with increasing operational complexity coupled with a diverse multi-stakeholder environment, servant leadership prevails as it puts followers first. Servant leadership not only put others first, it empowers people. In fact, empirical research by Kenneth E. Rauch (2007) and William R. Auxie (2013) in their doctoral dissertation on Servant Leadership found strong significant relationship between servant leadership, reduction in both absenteeism and attrition as well as improvement in sales performance in businesses (Indiana Wesleyan University, Department of Graduate Studies in Leadership and Graduate Program in Leadership PhD, Andrews University).

With honesty, excellent charisma and a positive attitude, good servant leaders are emotionally intelligent and have the capacity to address multiple concerns. **They aim to raise the overall well-being of their organization, family and businesses by serving and empowering people.** People are the centre of everything and leadership needs to pay attention to nurturing them. People are the largest single cost in most businesses. People are the largest, most valuable asset any company could have. All executive plans and business operations are carried out, or fail to be carried out, by people.

Good leadership means effective knowledge of processes or operations; of running the systems and resources efficiently. **Although first-class training, an incisive mind, and an endless supply of good ideas are useful asset, great leaders need self-awareness, self-regulation, motivation, empathy, and social skills. These qualities sound unbusinesslike, yet they are the hallmarks of great leaders.** And we found this to be embodied in servant leadership as lived and demonstrated by Jesus Christ. Because servant leadership operates a bottom-up model, they also have an effective problem distillation approach where they are able to identify issues and troubleshoot adequately.

Servant leadership is visionary leadership. Servant leaders are most appropriately positioned at seeing things with their followers or operating team and are capable to approach situations together with them rather than just merely delegating and not being involved in the problem-solving process. Because of their nature of being constantly engaged (face-to-face, one-on-one) with their team members, servant leaders by design usually have access to primary information (which they gather themselves) and not secondary handed-down information. Access to primary information either of the business or people is what makes a servant leader unique. And because of this hands-on approach it is safe to say that servant leaders possess some certain degree of analytical and technical skill required for success in what they do.

So we encourage you to aim to become a servant leader. Emulate the life and leadership of Jesus Christ. Jesus Christ attended to people in love and put others before himself. He enriched their lives. He was also excellent in

Kingdom business and operation. He lived it and had a perfect knowledge of the issues that could arise and was committed and empowered to solving them.

Contrary to the impression that you will be disrespected or looked down on, anecdotal evidences have shown that this type of leadership truly works and is most attractive. It makes the leader look good while at the same time builds up the team. Businesses that implore them have less employee turnover. The amazing thing is that good leadership can be cultivated and strengthened. We delve into this in another section of this book.

Reflection Points:
What leadership style are you operating with? How do you feel about your knowledge of the people that you work with, the ones that report to you and other downlines? What about your knowledge of the operation? Can you do an effective problem distillation and troubleshoot issues or concerns? Being a servant leader can help.

Personal Action and Development:
Start with daily practice to become a servant leader if you're not already one. In the beginning it may look silly but over time you will appreciate the value it will bring to you and those around you. Start with simple things like going for a break time with your direct reports or associates. Set a specific course of things that make you connect more to both your people and your process or operation.

RELATIONSHIPS ARE ESSENTIAL IN LIFE. BE RESPONSIBLE FOR MAKING IT WORK. NURTURE GOOD ONES, WEED OUT BAD ONES.

"Do nothing out of selfish ambition or vain conceit. Rather, in humility value others above yourselves" (Philippians 2:3). "Be of the same mind one toward another. Mind not high things, but condescend to men of low estate. Be not wise in your own conceits" (Romans 12:10, 16). "Two are better than one, because they have a good return for their labor" (Ecclesiastes 4:9).

BECOME MORE RELATABLE

Relationship is a touchy subject. We all know. Little wonder at one point that Facebook thought of including "complicated" as one of the relationship status options. With all of today's terminologies like "You-Economy", "Independent Business Owner", "Lone Wolf", "One Man Army" and so on, we are made to feel like we are more important than others. We have the impression that we don't need other people and that we can run our thing all by ourselves. Even "entrepreneurship" has now been confused for the term: "I do my own thing". But that is not the truth.

Jesus Christ the saviour of the world, who knew exactly what to do, how to do it and in fact had the power to do it, didn't go ahead to do it all by himself. He built relationships. Jesus Christ built the Church on relationships. He established a team. He invested in his team. We studied most of the top performing companies over the years, from Apple (Jobs & Wozniak, to Facebook (Zuckerberg & other co-founders), Google (Page & Brin), and so on. One core thing we found was that these companies started or thrived on the relationships the founders had with other people.

While individual resolve, believe in oneself and determination to accomplish something substantial in life is key to success, if we however desire to see our accomplishments sustained over the years, if we want to reach more people and make lasting impacts, we have to learn to work with others. Relationships are they key.

People are central to all that we do and the ability to develop interpersonal skills and work collaboratively with others is not only essential for personal success, it is top on the list of skills sought after in resume of job applicants all over the world. The reasons are obvious, people with poor interpersonal or relationship skills bring negative attitudes to the organization and could demoralize others.

Here, we will share our "Top 12 becoming a more relatable person ideas." We developed these points based on personal applications in our own context. We have found it to be applicable to many relationship contexts:

1. **Embrace the richness and diversity in others.** This could be a tough one especially when it comes to religious barriers we have placed over each other. But when we see each with the eyes of grace and embrace the uniqueness in others, such attitude become the foundational piece for those that truly want to thrive in whatever occupation or career they find themselves.

2. **Be willing to have sincere conversations.** What I have realized in my short life is that conversations that bring about action, change or results can sometimes come heated. To make relationships work and for us to benefit from it we have to learn to have hard conversations. More importantly, in heated argument our objective is to ensure that we don't lose our temper.

3. **Always give out a helping hand.** Always pitch in no matter the task. Our hands are meant to be extended in a helpful way; it is why we have arms and elbows! We are designed to do the work, hug each other, and extend a helpful hand.

4. **Be humble.** I am not talking of keeping quiet always. We can be ambitious, enthusiastic, and the very best in what we do, but balanced with a strong sense that we don't view ourselves as better than anyone else. We found an idea called "confidently humble" as we study the life of Moses. Regarded as the most humble man on the face of

the earth (Number 12:3) yet he was described as the man who God revealed Himself to (Numbers 12:5-8) and the one who confronted Pharaoh headlong to let God's people go. That you are confident in your skills and ability doesn't necessarily mean you are proud. Be confident (in Christ) yet, be humble. Sadly, true humility is fast diminishing in our modern day even though we are beginning to see that humility brings great gain.

5. **Be honest.** Honestly opening up about your strengths and weaknesses can be disarming to others in a group. Coming to the table with an honest view of yourself and of your shortcomings puts others at ease and creates a richer, more productive environment for all.

6. **Smile always.** Create an environment where people will find safe to be in. Not fake smile. Authentic, heart-warming smile coming from a reassuring heart that releases peace, hope and tranquility into the atmosphere. When people are in your space or you share space with people, lighting them up with your smile. It works magic and can be the only thing that person need to get by that day.

7. **Look at people in the face when talking to them.** The face is the seat of emotions. We can pick non-verbal ques, feel other's heart and be more relatable when we look people in the face. Don't look down or sideways when talking with people. (This could be especially difficult for those raised in Africa and some parts of Asia taught to always respect our elders :).

8. **Listen more and talk less.** Maybe that is why we have two ears and one mouth. And listening doesn't mean unnecessary quietness in front of others. It is being present in a communication exchange and ensuring that you provide attentive audience.

9. **Be a person of integrity.** Integrity is something really scarce today. While it is about the hardest, it is one of the most important in building good relationships. We discuss this more in a subsequent section of this book.

10. **Avoid gossips and other non-constructive talks about others.** Negatively talking about others behind them creates the impression that you can talk about just anyone behind them. And that kills trust. (Hint: to curb gossips be around highly productive people. They have less time to gossip).

11. **Be patient with others, especially difficult people.** While relationships are built on certain level of expectations, we should learn to cut others a slack and give grace even when they don't meet our expectations. We are all human. We are changing, evolving and getting better. But we need to ensure this is not allowing others become detrimental to our own personal growth.

12. **Focus on complementarity not competition.** Avoid unhealthy competition and strive within your relationships. Always recognize that everyone has a unique contribution to make. Focus on your unique calling. Develop yourself in it. Complement what others lack as they complement you too.

As we continue to learn more about relationships over the years, we came up with a relationship tenet and we believe it will help you as you continue to focus on building good relationships. You can write it somewhere to use as a benchmark and review as you go into different relationships. Also ensure to share with your friends and close acquaintances so you can together aspire for better growth-oriented relationships. Here is the relationship tenet:

"In my relationship, I want to constantly be challenged to get better. We are vision oriented. Integrity is our watchword. Our focus should be forward-looking. The atmosphere we create must be affirming and encouraging. We desire to often be out of our comfort zones and explore the learning zone. We want to meet each other with excitement. Failure is not our enemy, we see it as part of the process. We are willing to have meaningful, sincere yet sometimes hard conversations. We all win together. We are all growing and advancing. We desire change for the better. Continuous growth is modeled and expected." (see Appendix 4 for this tenet)

How about dealing with toxic relationships? It is important to know when to exit toxic relationships. When a relationship does not meet one or more of the relationship tenet earlier discussed (e.g. you are not growing or being challenged to get better. Or you are not excited or are always in your comfort zone, etc), it may be a good time to re-evaluate that relationship. Recognize that while we wish to have long-term relationship, some relationships are just meant to be short-term acquaintances. In the sections below, you will get to see how when you become a visionary, some of the price for following through your God-given vision (constrictionary properties of vision) is loss of "friends" that do not have any relevance in what God has shown you and/or what God will be doing in your future. Situations and circumstances do change beyond what we can handle and we need to let go of them. Your letting go is not an indication of pride or ego; it is simply an opportunity to move in the direction of a higher calling (in Christ). Even if you break out of ignorance, truly good relationships have a way of healing and sustaining itself over the years and through time.

As we conclude, we want you to know that not only do the company we keep say a lot about who we are, relationships can determine a lot more ranging from income level, health, spiritual growth, etc. This is one statement we heard recently that stuck with us: **"If you find yourself to be the best within your group, don't stay too long there. Find another group that will challenge you and help you grow"** Keep in mind what Jim Rohn said, "You are the average of the five people you spend the most time with." Les Brown put it in a way that is quiet succinct: "Your income is only $2K to $3K away from the income of your close friends." Relationship is key!

Reflection Points:

How do you feel about your relationships? Do they fall in line with some of the tenets of relationships? Do you feel like you are always the only one pushing for growth in your relationships? You may want to consider looking for other people that can challenge you to growth. Do you feel you are the one being encouraged to do better? Why not take this as an opportunity to yield? How about going through the "Top 12 becoming a more relatable person ideas" again and see which part you can do better on?

Personal Action and Development:

So this was basically how some of the points discussed here were developed: through practice. We both go to our respective offices each day or week and decided to practice one or more of the "Top 12 becoming a more relatable person ideas". For example, at a point we would offer a helping hand on or project. For another example, we choose to practice listening more to our colleagues when they are talking or during meetings. Being the one listening could be harder to do as a leader, but make the effort still. It's not surprising to see that when something broke or a colleague is feeling sad, some of them could confide in us. Others just find it comfortable to join us for a minute walk to calm down and come back in shape during a high intense work day in the office. What we are basically saying is that it takes practice and consistent effort to build good relationships. You could also give it a try yourself and see how much progress you make with your relationships. But we have to be sensitive to always check it against a good relationship tenet so that what we call a good relationship is not actually a bad one. If you notice your relationships is not in line with one or two of the points we shared in the relationship tenet it may be a good idea to re-evaluate that relationship(s) by taking each point in the tenet and asking are we in line or not.

THERE IS POWER IN SOLITUDE; THE QUIET AND STILL SOUL ALLOWS FOR THE ORGANIC GROWTH OF EMPIRICAL TRUTH.

Psalm 46:10 says, "Be still, and know that I am God. "Jesus, "often withdrew to lonely places and prayed" (Luke 5:16), spending time alone with His Father. We see Him seeking out solitude after performing miracles (Mark 1:35), in times of grief (Matthew 14:13), before choosing the twelve apostles (Luke 6:12–13), in His distress in Gethsemane (Luke 22:39–44), and at other times. Solitude was a consistent practice in Jesus' life.

THE POWER OF SOLITUDE

There is so much going on in our world today. From the phone ringing and pinging to the TV screen filled with lots of latest happenings, it appears that there's no time to pause, meditate and rejuvenate. There suddenly appear to be so many unfinished projects hanging around our necks. Feelings get mixed up and we begin to wonder if we will end up as a failure or success. This calls for some time of solitude – for effective reflection and meditation. Whether we evaluate ourselves to have failed or succeeded is really not the issue. What should matter is what we do with the failure or success experience in future. And this is where the place of solitude comes in. Solitude in this context is not a bad thing. It is not the type known as solitary confinement or incarceration which is usually accompanied with torture, agony and pain.

Undoubtedly, we need others: friends, associates, family and close acquaintances around us, but as individuals we need moments where we get to be alone. Solitude in this context is quality time of reflection and meditation. Finding a place of solitude and quietness is most crucial at specific times and seasons of our lives. Solitude can be triggered by external factors or it can be internally activated. Some may call it quiet time. Some may call it personal retreat. It could be a long one. It could be short. What you do to activate the moment can differ from one to another but the end result are usually the same. Solitude moments illuminates and refreshes us as we take some time out to regurgitate various information that we have been exposed to; processing them more slowly to tap all the available nutrient and value we can derive. The inner reflection that occurs in the place of solitude is what helps clarify our perspectives and give new, deeper meaning to things we have heard and seen.

I first conceptualized this idea of tapping power in the place of solitude about a decade and half ago when I learnt the "Cabinet Meeting" principle taught by Prof. J.K. Oloke. A renowned scientist, professor Oloke's ground breaking career in Fermentation Technology and Medical Biotechnology can only be attributed to something extraordinary. He explained, **"In the cabinet meeting you have God the Father, God the Son and God the Holy Spirit present…imagine them sitting at a table with you…The trinity being present."**

You can further imagine solitude as a chemical fractional distillation process (see Appendix 3 for a hypothetical Power of Solitude Fractional Distillation diagram). Imagine our minds being in laboratory set up containing mixtures. We allow the Holy Spirit to breath on us to the point of condensing out impurities so that the final result will be pure thoughts or results.

Although meditation is not the only thing that happens during solitude moments (praying, communing with God, etc also occur here), meditation however has a strong connection to what we do in the place of Solitude. Meditating on the truth, the word of God, is definitely a sure thing in the place of solitude. And medical scientists have extensively unraveled how powerful meditation can be.

Rebecca Gladding, M.D. (co-author of *You Are Not Your Brain*, a clinical instructor and attending psychiatrist at UCLA), reports that meditation helps withering of the connection between the body's sensation and fear centres and the area of the brain's prefrontal cortex that is involved in processing information related to you and people you perceive as being similar to you. This decreases your tendency to think that something is wrong and that you are problem. As a result, anxiety levels tend to go down. She further added that meditation helps you "look at things from a more rational, logical and balanced perspective".

The eventual outcome of the power of solitude is that your brain also forms a stronger bond between your bodily sensations and the part of the brain's prefrontal cortex that processes information about people who we see as different from us, which boosts our ability for empathy and for evaluating situations from someone else's perspective. This ultimately leads to what has been generally referred to as **"your moral compass,"** which improves your people skills, another key professional asset. Even more, meditation comes with the rewarded of greater problem-solving abilities, better ideas, and, potentially, important breakthroughs.

Effectively communing with God, reflecting on His word, and meditating in the place of solitude allows us to build content knowledge and expertise. We can't say it too much: **there is power in solitude; the quiet and still soul allows for the organic growth of empirical truth.** Maximizing the power of solitude allows for the truth (in God's word) and wisdom (of good people around us, good books we read, etc.) to grow organically in us. Maximizing the power of solitude requires meditation. In the place of solitude, we put an experience or encounter of life into the slow cooker of our heart and allow grace and fresh breath on it. **Positive solitude activates illumination and the ultimate end result is GROWTH.**

Solitude was a consistent practice in Jesus' life and learning from Him we wrap up with this key idea: before any action, practice solitude. After every action, a solitude moment is required. Whether the outcome of an action was positive or negative, practice solitude. Although it may first appear like time wasted, with practice, we found out that the result of solitude moments are effective actions that have been clearly thought through. So it is not time wasted, it is time invested. Everyone that exercises that power of solitude will find it to be a powerful instrument in their decision-making toolbox.

Reflection Points:

Trust us when we tell you that catching moments of solitude can be tough. We both work full-time in downtown Toronto, have a toddler, run multiple small businesses and are highly involved in our community. Yet we know how crucial pausing momentarily can be in maintaining success and ensuring sustainability in all that God has done and is doing in our lives. Solitude doesn't have to be characterized by going on a distant journey to look for a place that is far from where people live. If you have the chance to do that - great! But solitude can be practiced anywhere. It has to do with learning to shut out noises and distraction and focusing on specific topics or subjects. Don't be talked into believing that it is only for older people or during problem times. Solitude is relevant whether small or big, a short moment or extended period of time. The most important thing is to learn to galvanize thoughts and put them in slow motion. You can invite the Holy Spirit to join in to make a meeting we call "Cabinet Meeting". We talk often, solitude moments can be the opportunity to listen more.

We also want to add that while further reflecting on the points we raised in this section, don't let your solitude moments result in analysis paralysis – a situation where you think about an issue to the point where there is no result or in fact you become worse off yourself. Solitude doesn't mean thinking about negative things or failure outcomes of a goal or project. In the place of Solitude, simply invite the third person in trinity – the Holy Spirit – to join in. How about staring with a heart full of worship and gratitude?

Personal Action and Development:

Try it today. Try it often. Take a line of thought, theory, assumption, information or hypothesis you heard from somewhere that you want the gain more clarity and insight into and go into solitude. Begin to demystify or do what we call "Fractional Distillation" by breaking every line of thoughts into small fractions or atomic unit. Please see the hypothetical "Fractional Distillation/Power of Solitude diagram" in Appendix 3 below.

Allow the Holy Spirit to minister deeper to you and help you through. Think long term. Think short term. Process information, break them apart, assemble them - all in the slow cooker of your heart and review the results. It's like a play, pause, rewind, and repeat process. You may not finish on a single line of though in one solitude moment. You can come back again. Do this until you feel good about what you have done, are doing or will do. If you feel good about it, go ahead and take action. If not, reflect further in solitude. Sometimes we may not still get clarity to a problem in solitude. You may need to seek help or further guidance.

THE DISCOURSE OF DEVELOPING LEADERSHIP QUALITIES IS NOT FOR A SELECTED FEW. EVERY SINGLE ONE OF US HAVE BEEN CALLED TO LEAD IN ONE FORM OR ANOTHER; NO MATTER WHO WE ARE OR WHERE WE ARE FROM.

We are reminded in Deuteronomy 28:13 that we are the head. Your horn has been exalted like that of a unicorn (Psalm 92:10). You are destined to stand before lead and stand before kings as you demonstrate excellence in what you do (Proverbs 22:29). Carry out your duties with dignity and not with mediocrity.

YOU ARE A LEADER

You are a leader. Someone reading this might say: "Unnmmm...I don't think I am." Well, the truth is by God's design every single one of us was created to excel and lead in at least one area of life. Each one of us is a masterpiece at something. Sadly, we didn't come to this realization early enough. It is important to note that despite being a leader in one area, you can be a follower or member elsewhere. But the key point is, **there is something you are unique at; you excel in one area of life than others. You are a leader.**

Many of us are burdened either historically or culturally by some version of leadership connected to a "Great Man" theory (well documented in Joseph C. Rost 1993 book: *Leadership for the Twenty-First Century*). The "Great Man" theory is built on the premise that leaders are wealthy, strong, muscular, male, 45 – 55yrs, extroverts, tall, big in stature with thousands and millions of followers. The "Great Man" theory further presupposes that leaders are the ones who make up the C-suite in the boardroom and the better looking the more successful they were.

The implication of thinking of leadership in the "Great Man" perspective is that ordinary people like ourselves and you are left feeling that demographically we are automatically disqualified to be leaders. Because of this marginalization, some begin to rely on intuition and a creative spark to get things done instead of gaining knowledge, confidence and owning the process or operation they are in charge of. Others choose to servitude rather than to lead; be overly introvertish and feel unnecessarily reserved instead of taking ownership for achieving outcomes. Many are left with the impression that they can never be leaders.

Our question need to change from "how do I measure up to this 'Great Man' archetype?" to "How can I lead effectively from where I am and with who I am?"

Leadership is a truly complex, sensitive and often misunderstood subject. But as Phanella Mayall Fine and Alice Olins put it in their book, *Step Up*, "Whether you like it or not, you're a leader." Let's make this clear. Although you may not label yourself as a leader, the fact that you influence someone, motivate another, are a visionary and are strategic or methodical (at least to some extent) in your execution, you are a leader. This type of niche leadership is now been referred to by some recent literatures as "micro-influencing". Micro-influencers are dubbed to have the ability to provide "micro-reach" and large companies are now been advised to engage multiple micro-influencers rather than one big-gun celebrity.

Fine and Olins further stressed that when we present ourselves as capable, willing future leaders (even if we're very happy not directing the Hollywood's next blockbuster movie) we single ourselves out as someone determined, capable, imaginative and confident. The crux of good leadership is not the number of people below us, it is how we're regarded and how we regard others. When you act like a leader - capably and with passion - it's hard to not motivate others in your wake.

It is true that it takes greater skill to manage bigger teams and larger organizations. It is also true that leadership is embedded in service, accountability and stewardship. These greater skills come with adequate training and equipping. As seeds of leadership are watered and developed, "micro-influencer" leaders become even more effective leaders.

That you are here today means you have a purpose. Whether you are called to lead a business organization, coordinate parking during a gathering, provide home care for children at home or appointed to lead a congregation, you have been called to leadership. Handle your task with poise, courage, commitment and determination.

So whatever you do, always raise the bar higher. Do it with excellence and courage. Be fervent in spirit. Your confidence will grow as you take one step at a time. As you build more confidence, others will regard and appreciate your leadership capabilities. Even if they don't, that you are in the position to influence younger ones around you still makes you a leader. So operate like one.

Let's wrap this up with the following observation on leadership we found in Peter Senge's book, *The Fifth Discipline*:
"Most of the outstanding leaders I've worked with are neither tall nor especially handsome; they are often mediocre public speakers; they do not stand out in a crowd; they do not mesmerize an attending audience with their brilliance or eloquence. Rather, what distinguishes them is the clarity and persuasiveness of their ideas, the depth of their commitment, and their openness to continually learning more."

So we conclude, leaders are not born, they're made. Leadership develops.

Reflection Points:
Which school of thoughts do you belong: that leaders are born or that leaders are made? One school of thought proposes that leaders are made from a select few unique individuals, born with a rare set of leadership abilities. The other school of thought stands on the premise that leaders are made, that we learn, grow and develop into leaders.

Warren Gamaliel Bennis, a leading American scholar, presidential adviser, organizational consultant and pioneer of contemporary leadership studies concludes that vast majority of leaders are made through focused effort, hard work and daily action. Again, which school of thought do you belong? Whether you are micro-influencing or have a larger sphere of influence, which school of thought do you belong to?

Let's extend this reflection point on leadership school of thought further. Can you make an effort to identify whether Jesus was born a leader or whether he learned/developed leadership? You could argue it both ways. His deity could have conferred automatic leadership on him divinely by birth. But being born as an ordinary man, the son of a carpenter, changes the entire narrative and points in the direction that he started from the scratch like myself and you. Jesus grew to the top through humility, service, sacrifices and all of the other traits we mentioned in this section and the other section on "Leadership Cure Many Things" were derived from the Biblical leadership of Jesus.

Personal Action and Development:
Ask your friends, family and peers what things you do very well? There are also certain things that you do that brings you a great sense of accomplishment. Take note of these things and make effort to develop yourself to do better in the areas mentioned. As you develop and work in these areas, your leadership capabilities grows. There is more to managing larger teams but growing in the little that you do and building on your area of core competency is a good start!

IT IS COSTLY TO ASSUME THAT GROWTH WILL HAPPEN BY ITSELF. TO TRULY GROW, WE HAVE TO TAKE RESPONSIBILITY FOR HOW WE GROW; ENSURING TO MEASURE AND CHECK OVER TIME IF IT IS IN THE RIGHT DIRECTION AND SUSTAINABLE.

In Genesis chapter 1 verses 4, 10, 12, 18, 21, 25 and 31 we see God pausing intermittently, reviewed the process of creation and said: "it was good!" Then he moved on to another piece of the task and finishing that also, He said "it was good!" We too can take responsibility for how we are growing, set specific measuring yardstick and pausing to review over time the direction and sustainability.

PERSONAL GROWTH: TAKE RESPONSIBILITY

Measuring growth, fine-tuning growth directions and making growth sustainable are processes that can sound quite ambiguous and overwhelming. The sad thing we wouldn't want to experience in life, however, is to take one step forward and later two steps backward. If that is the case, we may end up being worse and rather than grow, we are retrogressing. That is why we have to take responsibility for our personal growth; ensuring that it is measurable and specific.

We need to be vigilant as we make progress. We need to constantly check if what we are calling growth is not actually a short-term quick fix that may not last. For example, how do you classify a real estate agent who religiously accompanies his family to church only because being perceived as a family oriented, God fearing man is "good for business." The real estate agent has completely designed his life around "getting ahead" in business and somehow managed to tangle the family, Church and community into that bracket. This should not be so. Many started out their businesses and careers with this "getting ahead" mentality – believing that they can fake righteousness living (going to church) in order to get a couple business referrals. The question we need to ask ourselves is this: looking at things holistically is it sustainable to only "get ahead" in business by manipulating our family, community, etc.?

The right perspective is to first understand that we are made divinely, to be the very best we can be in whatever we intend to do. All that we need for life and godliness is already available to us in sufficiency (2 Peter 1:3). Greatness is already inside of us. We only need to nurture it. We have been divinely endowed with creative abilities. We only need to develop it. We are not supposed to force our way to "get ahead" so much so that we tangle our family, church and community into it. By so doing we are not living to fullness and would hardly have genuine rest. So going to Church with our family is the right direction but doing it only for business related purposes may not make it sustainable. Doing it to be a better father or mother, to be the best person we can be, is how to sustain it. It is the ethical part of the whole process that offers a meaningful framework resulting in purpose, a strong sense of self-esteem [based on Christ-esteem] and direction. The ethical part includes consideration first for ourselves and then to our family members and work, business associates or Church.

Having a right perspective and being ethical applies to life in general. Our motive for careers and jobs, companies to work for, mentors to learn from and so on shouldn't be based out of just desire to make money or "get ahead". We have to take responsibility for our growth which sometimes means sacrificing comfort and lucratively trading certainty for opportunity to learn and grow.

Personal development and growth shouldn't just be a goal, it should be a lifestyle. It should be an habit that everything we do in life filters through. Taking charge of your own growth is so rewarding. When we learn how to take responsibility for our growth, we strengthen our confidence and overall outcome in life. So start right now. Make sure whatever you want to experience growth in is measurable, has direction and is sustainable.

Reflection Points:
Sustainability requires careful planning. Isn't it high time we stop waking up daily and not have a life plan? Set up a plan and work through it. Failing to plan is planning to fail. Planning our growth journey helps us to mindfully take stock and be focused. It also increases our self-awareness

84

and is a powerful personal development technique. Come to think of it, if you don't take responsibility for your personal growth, who will? Not a complete list, some ways to experience growth could include: Taking a course or enrolling in a program, reaching out for mentorship, etc. You can record your personal progress in a journal.

Personal Action and Development:

We strongly recommend having a growth journal or writing pad. Please don't join those that conclude that journals are for kids only. Keep a journal yourself. Document virtually anything in your journal. Document people, places, encounters, ideas, etc. along the growth journey. It is our own growth journal that actually gave birth to this book you are reading right now. No serious organization or structure needed in the journaling. There is nobody to impress upon, nobody to fool either. So just keep to your innermost emotions and thought about what is going on in your life. Set specific measuring yardsticks and review over time.

EMBRACE CRITICISM; SEE THEM AS TOOLS TO HELP YOU GET BETTER ESPECIALLY WHEN THEY COME FROM PEOPLE WHO MEAN GOOD AND ARE INTERESTED IN YOUR OVERALL WELLBEING.

Galatians 2:11-21 Paul criticized peter. Believers followed Peter's hypocrisy. They were not following the truth of the gospel message. It is important to note that not all criticism come with the right motive but there are certain people that we should accept their criticism because they want the best for us.

EMBRACE CONSTRUCTIVE CRITICISM

In the book, *Reminiscences of Abraham Lincoln by Distinguished Men of His Time* – Edited by Allen Thorndike Rice, there was an interesting event that unravelled between President Abraham Lincoln and Secretary of War Edwin Stanton. During the Civil War, President Lincoln signed an order to transfer certain regiments, but Secretary of War Edwin Stanton refused to execute it, calling the president a fool. When Lincoln heard, he replied, "If Stanton said I was a fool, then I must be one, for he is nearly always right, and generally says what he means. I will step over..." The President did, and when Stanton convinced him the order was in error, Lincoln quietly withdrew it. Part of Lincoln's greatness lay in his ability to rise above pettiness, ego, and sensitivity to other people's opinions. He wasn't easily offended. He masterfully handled criticism and in doing so demonstrated one of the strengths of a truly great person: humility.

We all don't like to get criticized. But how do we get better if we don't expose what we do to be assessed by others especially by our close subordinates? The question should therefore be how do we handle good criticisms and how can we use them to become a better team member or leader with results in overall effectiveness of our personal lives, organization and businesses?

When it comes to constructive criticism, the first thing to be conscious of is the motive and the intended end result. The end result should be to make us better; growth. Sometimes it can come through heated conversations, experiences has shown that it is sometimes those who are very concerned about us or the operation concerned that will get really passionate. So we shouldn't be surprised when even well-meaning people come to us in a rather unexpectedly hard tone. We shouldn't be distracted by the medium through which criticism is delivered. **We should learn to filter through the noise and access the wisdom we can gain.** Our focus should be to learn from constructive criticism and grow wiser. Embrace criticism; see them as a tool to help you get better especially when they come from people who mean good and are interested in your overall wellbeing. Sure, there are unjustified, destructive criticism. But we are reminded not to be rebellious or find ways to out-argue or counter-argue claims and accusations brought against us. It could be a hard thing to do in the moment, but remember that this is a call to appropriating values and creating a whole new positive paradigm to how you or others would have previously responded.

Don't give in to resentment or striking back. Just like Paul criticized Peter for leading believers hypocritically, we too must be prepared for such. They were not following the truth of the gospel message. Even Jesus was criticized too, so you're in good company. If criticism get negative and destructive, remember never to sin or be deceitful. Be patient. God has called us to do good and just as Christ suffered, he serve as our example today (1 Peter 2:20-23 NLT).

Reflection Points:
Have you been criticized? How did you handle it? When we are faced with criticism, do you agree that it is wise to be patient and filter through the points to discover which one will be useful for personal development (growth) and which ones are mere negative destructive criticism? Chances are that there are certain people that criticize with grace and their criticism could be an opportunity to become a better person. We stumbled on a quote on twitter (via @leadershipcures handle) that really got us thinking. You can further reflect on it too. Here it is: "If feedback is the

breakfast of champions why is it hard to swallow?"
Something to think about right?

Personal Action and Development:
Write out below what you think your line of action
should be when you get criticized whether constructively or
not. We strongly recommend you do actually write below as
a process of memorizing and internalizing what your
response would be when you are criticized constructively or
otherwise.

TRAVEL EXPERIENCES CAN CHANGE YOUR LIFE. IT'S WHEN YOU TAKE JOURNEYS AND STEP OUT OF YOUR COMFORT ZONE THAT YOUR EYES ARE OPENED TO THE BEAUTY AND BLESSEDNESS OF ALL THAT GOD HAS CREATED.

In Genesis 1 we see how God made all things and in verse 31 He exclaimed: "it was very good!" It doesn't matter how we look at it, the world is beautiful. Traveling around the world we get to see the beauty of what God has created comes to life! Places, people, food and cultures. A single travel experience changed our lives and we know it can change yours too!

TAKE A JOURNEY, EXPAND YOUR HORIZON, LEARN AND GROW

As contradictory as it may sound, without traveling out of the place where you are from and lived all your life, you can't truly appreciate that same place. Your ability to step out of that location and experience what others have and you don't and vice versa ultimately results in your overall appreciation of that very location.

Say for example you lived all your life in a city where the transportation system is primarily cars and street cars, you will be fascinated when you get to another city where biking is their primary means of transportation. **When we travel, not only do we truly appreciate the place where we are from, we also get to correct false beliefs and opinions about certain places or people.** Our cultural sensitivity is developed. Above all, we are exposed to new learning experience, opportunities and possibilities.

Personal experiences help to correct false opinions or made-up, cooked-up realities. Falling into the group of people holding false opinions can be very easy. It just takes two to three people to carry around the same message and before long it becomes a generally accepted and valid assertion. Having first-hand experience of cultures enhances our cultural sensitivity – a vital personal quality in our fast globalizing world. Travelling exposes us to underlying values that may explain certain behavioral traits common with a group of people. This therefore produces the opportunity for you to grow your friendships/networks as well as deepen existing relationships.

Travelling enlightens us about so many other things in our world including people's attitudes, food culture, cultural behavior, differences in fashion, lifestyle trends and much more. In its most effective form, traveling exposes us to great learning opportunities and challenges us to grow and get better in any particular area we find most relevant or challenging.

The most important aspect of traveling is how we get to know even ourselves better. The challenges, opportunities, exposures, education, on-the-road, out-of-comfort-zone into-the-learning-zone experiences helps us discover who we are. If you're open and willing, travel will make you an incredibly better-rounded human being. And that should actually be the goal after all.

Our personal story was such that we both found each other in the UK (Europe) while studying. Having come from two different continents: Africa and North America and with roots in the Caribbean and trips to South America. Our family could only have been formed through traveling and meeting each other in Hull UK. We have come to know the blessedness of traveling.

And when you return from a trip, the opportunity to share really interesting stories with friends gives a sense of accomplishment. After experiencing places with names that everyone around you cannot pronounce, there is nothing more to feel than a sense of growth and accomplishment among your peers. Adding a little humor makes it even more fun and rewarding.

Travel enhances your biodiversity index (human and other animal species) with resulting positive impact on your communication on both business and personal levels.

In Philippians 2:4 (NIV) we read that 'Each of you should look not only to your own interests but also to the interests of others.'

So don't be self-absorbed –go for a trip!

Reflection Points:

Come to think of it, most of what we know about other parts of the world are presented to us through the media: TV, prints, books, etc. To a large extent, we saw the world through other people's eye and not ours. What if what we have heard, read, or seen through these media is a fraction of what the reality is? What if some of them were totally wrong? Do you appreciate the need for first-hand information that validates and authenticates what we have heard before? Do you see why traveling is good?

Personal Action and Development:

Plan a trip before the end of the year. Explore a new city, country, continent, society or culture. Take note of new friends, or people you meet. Try something adventurous!

IT'S OK FOR PEOPLE NOT TO BELIEVE IN YOU BUT IT'S WORST FOR YOU NOT TO BELIEVE IN YOURSELF. CHRIST IN YOU IS THE HOPE OF GREATNESS.

Jesus made a resounding statement to the father of the ailing boy: "Anything is possible if a person believes." (Mark 9:23). Believing first in God and his only son Jesus Christ (John 14:1) activates the dynamic and powerful Holy Spirit in you (2 Corinthians 1:21-22). With this, you can do what improbable people call impossible. Only believe.

SELF-ESTEEM IS GOOD, CHRIST-ESTEEM IS THE BEST

Self-esteem or self-confidence, as some call it, is good. It is rooted in self-believe. It's the biggest difference noticeable between successful people and unsuccessful people. Beyond intelligence, opportunity and resources, just believing in oneself can make goals achievable. Believing in oneself helps to overcome vulnerability, uncertainty, and failure that is ever so besetting us. **And when we say self-esteem we don't mean "ruthless" self-awareness.** We don't recommend this type of obsessive consciousness of yourself. The "ruthless" obsessive type of self-esteem is usually accompanied by a rigorous commitment to self-examination and course correction: not in pursuit of an archetype but in an effort to be the best "you" you could be. Obsessive self-consciousness is not good.

It is key to note however, that if you don't believe that it's possible to make new things work, if you lack the confidence, then it's hard to make any progress. It doesn't matter how good the ideas are, nothing will work for you if you don't believe in it. And more importantly, nothing will work if you don't believe in yourself. The type of confidence we need is the type that comes from within, from the deep belief in ourselves and our abilities.

To truly believe in yourself, as 'touchy-feely' as this may sound, you need to have someone that first believed in you. Someone who will be the pillar and backbone for you in all your endeavours. Great leaders can do this for their protégé. We have enjoyed the privilege of great men and women who have supported us and stood with us through our journey. We are grateful.

But we also know the very one, Jesus Christ, who is the sine qua non - the "without which, not" - of success. God is sovereign, omnipotent and omniscient, loving and unchanging. Through Christ God demonstrates His commitment to our ultimate triumph and success which led to the cross. So we can trust in Him. Christ is the perfect reflection of greatness whose Spirit can dwell in us to bring about an assurance or confidence that is firm and solid. **The confidence that comes from the Holy Spirit within gravitates us from self-esteem to the unfailing and unwavering Christ-esteem.**

Romans 8:15-16 puts it this way: "For you did not receive a spirit of slavery to fall back into fear, but you received the Spirit of adoption, by whom we cry out, "Abba, Father!" The Spirit Himself testifies together with our spirit that we are God's children. Galatians 4:4-7 emphasizes that "God sent His Son, born of a woman, born under the law, to redeem those under the law, so that we might receive adoption as sons. And because you are sons, God has sent the Spirit of His Son into our hearts, crying, "Abba, Father!" So you are no longer a slave, but a son; and if a son, then an heir through God. Philippians 4:13 says "I can do all things through Christ which strengtheneth me." Isaiah 41:10 – "Fear thou not; for I [am] with thee: be not dismayed; for I [am] thy God: I will strengthen thee; yea, I will help thee; yea, I will uphold thee with the right hand of my righteousness." **So let your faith drown your fear and let it strengthen your confidence and ignite your passion and drive.**

Yes the world is full of uncertainty and unpredictability but those of us that live by faith and put our trust in God live above fear of uncertainty. We have the assurance of a great future and evidences of things not seen. In Hebrews 11:1 we read: "Now faith is the substance of things hoped for, the evidence of things not seen."

You need to shore up your confidence because a major piece of life secret's success, "the mystery" is now being made known to you and that is: "Christ in you is the hope of glory". Colossians 1:27 declares: "For God wanted them to know that the riches and glory of Christ are for you Gentiles, too. And this is the secret: Christ lives in you. This gives you the assurance of sharing his glory." The practical implication of this type of confidence is to say this to yourself: "I am handing over myself to Christ and allowing Jesus take the lead. I am stepping out of the way and letting Christ go instead. I am letting Jesus off the bench and get Him working in my life."

So build your confidence level in Christ because if you are not confident enough, you'll break like a twig the first time you face an obstacle. Maybe some of us are already facing obstacles right now. Whatever you want to achieve, there will be countless barriers questioning your competency. The only way to get through these barriers is by being confident and believing enough that you can and will overcome. But confidence takes a whole new, higher level when we have the Holy Spirit empowering and giving us the boldness we need for every aspect of our lives. That is Christ-esteem at work! This Christ-esteem has worked for us and most assuredly the confidence we have in this Live Love Learn Grow project. It can work for you too. Only believe.

Reflection Points:
Be honest, you had the impression that "self-confidence" is all about you right? The truth is somebody, a bigger and more powerful entity have to be our source of inner courage and strength. Psychology taught us that certain behavioural patterns can help us live and lead effectively. The guarantee that these behavioural theories or assumptions will work is a vast and complex as the number of propositions or assumption surrounding humanity itself.

That is why we absolutely believe that Christ-esteem is the mother of true self-esteem.

Personal Action and Development:
List some current life situations below that you appear to be lacking self-esteem or confidence in. Read through some of the scriptures above as well as others you find in scriptures and put them in from of those life situations listed. For example, if you are facing a new job routine and the context is: "This new task is too daunting I am a little afraid" as a response apply Isaiah 41:10 - "I will fear not. God will strengthen and help me. He will uphold me with his right hand"

JUST LIKE AN EMPTY SAC WILL TAKE THE SHAPE OF WHEREVER IT IS PLACED, IF YOU ARE NOT STANDING FOR SOMETHING, YOU WILL INADVERTENTLY FALL FOR ANYTHING.

"…Choose you this day whom you will serve; whether the gods which your fathers served that were on the other side of the flood, or the gods of the Amorites, in whose land you dwell: but as for me and my house, we will serve the LORD" (Joshua 24:15). "Wherefore take unto you the whole armour of God, that ye may be able to withstand in the evil day, and having done all, to stand (Ephesians 6:13). "Stand fast therefore in the liberty wherewith Christ hath made us free…" (Galatians 5:1).

STAND FOR SOMETHING IN LIFE

Joshua put forward a crucial charge at a crucial time in the life of the Children of Israel in Joshua 24:15. It wasn't long after Moses passed on that the people got carried away by many other things that appear to be taking their attention from the one key thing that is most crucial: love for God. Their love for idols has fast replaced their heart of service. They appear to have been quietly nursing and being enchanted by things, creations of God, rather than God Himself. And He presented them with a charge that requires their own free will or choice.

In our contemporary time, idols have fast metamorphosed into mundane things. We live in a world carried away by fads and fashion, things that don't last. We want quick fixes and constantly new experiences albeit in the wrong ways. We are always looking for the next new gig. Many travel far, not with a growth or learning intention as we mentioned earlier in this book but just for mere pleasure and the satisfaction of ulterior motives. This takes them even further away from God. We are all human and our longing for pleasure and personal gratification digs an even deeper well of dissatisfaction causing us to toss back and forth without any grounded footing in purpose and meaning.

It is okay to keep searching, and while searching, have a value orientation. Experimentation here and there is in order, a few trial and errors, before we ultimately find our true purpose. But when we hop around aimlessly after the fashion and trends in town, we end up being on the receiving end. We need to move from being an end receiver to becoming creative contributors and actors in the events of life. We need to take responsibility and start playing active roles in contributing significantly both to ourselves and others around us.

This discussion applies to the young people of today as well as the older generation. We all have to make our choices. When young people take a stand in Christ early in life, they quickly build experience along their divine, original pathways. Standing for something early in life allows young people to overcome and equip themselves with more tools to defeat the enemy as they journey on in life. Together with the excellence and leadership we build along the way, we inevitably become champions of worthy causes in our community.

When older people take a stand in Christ, they prevent their families from degenerating spiritually. When people who are mature take their stand like Joshua, they raise their family in purpose and as a blessing to their community.

More importantly, to take a stand, you need to really know who you are. You need to know that God made you and formed you. Know that he pre-ordained your life and has designed something great for you. Don't settle with mediocre people who don't aim for excellence. You have been designed to be the head, to shine as light and to preserve like salt. So rise up today and be outstanding. Don't fall for just anything and everything. Stand for something.

Reflection Point:
Do you see yourself following everything happening around you to the point where it has become an obsession that you must wear, buy, use or be in tune with virtually everything in vogue? Are you among the set of people who insists that some celebrities are their model and they will do anything to become like them? Check and see whether you have a true identity for yourself? Do you need to find deeper meaning and purpose today? Those that accept the supremacy of Christ and follow in his saving grace and

power usually command attention too. Some are just too humble or quiet for you to hear them. They are influencing and leading others to find their own purpose in Christ. So do you want to take your stand or re-affirm your stand by re-enacting your faith? Today is your day!

Personal Action and Development:

Enumerate the last few items you purchased and see what influenced you to buying them. Were they needs or you merely purchased because your friends are doing in to maintain their class in the "reigning club". Take a moment and reflecting on how you derive meaning for yourself? Is it through things you possess or through the one God who lives in you? Outline what you plan to do to take a new stand (you have not done so) or to maintain your godly stand e.g. I will tell my friends that I have to attend a skill development workshop or Bible study instead of the next all night party?

TWO PROFOUND THINGS OCCURRED AT CALVARY: MERCY FOR THE PAST AND GRACE FOR A VICTORIOUS FUTURE. WE BEAR PROOF OF THESE WHEN WE CARRY THE CROSS DAILY.

"You see, at just the right time, when we were still powerless, Christ died for the ungodly. Very rarely will anyone die for a righteous person, though for a good person someone might possibly dare to die. But God demonstrates his own love for us in this: While we were still sinners, Christ died for us."(Romans 5:6-8) "for this is how God loved the world: he gave his one and only son, so that everyone who believes in him will not perish but have eternal life. (John 3:16). "The message of the cross is foolish to those who are headed for destruction! But we who are being saved know it is the very power of God." (1 Corinthians 1:18).

THE POWER OF THE CROSS

While discussions surrounding the Cross and Calvary could be an overwhelmingly complicated subject even to theologians, we found it to be the core for any sustainable growth experience in our own lives. Despites its complexity, a clear understanding of the cross is especially crucial for a victorious Christian living in our modern day. We need to be solidified in the truth in order to stand the test that times and seasons are posing against us; both in our lives and by direct effects on our businesses and daily endeavours.

We are humans and we are mortal. All of us have at times been defeated by Satan (Romans 5:8). We are held in bondage to sin and are controlled by the power of the devil. We have come to learn that the cross is the instrument by which God delivers us from the penalty of our sins and from the hand of Satan. To live in freedom above sin, fear or reproach and to experience true peace and productivity, we have to acknowledge what Christ did on the cross and thereby appropriate the power of the cross in our daily endeavours. For us to be successful in our lives and to experience fruitfulness in our businesses, we need to understand the purpose and effectiveness of the cross. That is the reason why we felt the need for it to be featured in this book. We are a living testimony of the power of the cross.

So let's look at it from this angle. Imagine that your dad was the chief judge – he institutionalizes the law and upholds it. Imagine that you violated the law and you were brought before the chief judge – your dad. Imagine that He spelt out the penalty for the offence you committed and by law it was a death sentence. Imagine that after your father pronounced the death sentence, he stood up from the chief judge's seat and declared that instead of you, he will pay the price and face the death sentence. How would you feel? I know it will feel sober at first but in the end, you get liberation and freedom.

You see, that was exactly what happened through the Calvary process – a process of the death and resurrection of Jesus Christ on the cross. Through this process, God came and intervened in the situations of humanity and declared us free once and for all. God atoned for us. His love and mercy prevailed. While the first and most important objective of Christ dying was for our sins and to cleanse us of all unrighteousness, many do not know that the forgiveness of our sins is not the end of the story. The benefits of the cross are much more. Not only has Jesus freed us from all condemnation, but we have a whole new identity, according to John 1:12 and 2 Corinthians 5:17. He has given us purpose, power, and hope to live here on Earth now! The power of the cross!

So the cross goes beyond just the jewelry we put on our body. While this is a good thing and a symbol of our faith, the power and effectiveness of the cross goes even deeper. In the cross we see the clearest evidence of the world's guilt. At the cross of Christ, sin reached its climax. Its most terrible display took place at Calvary. It was never blacker nor more hideous. We see the human heart laid bare and its corruption fully exposed. The Scripture teaches that man's heart is desperately wicked. But God hates sin. And in the cross we see the strongest proof of God's hatred of sin (Ezekiel 18:20; Romans 6:23).

The cross is a symbol of out sinful nature as human (the very height of it), yet, through it, God's pours out his greatest love towards all of us. Covering for the past, the present and the future.

Mercy for the past to cover our tyranny of sin and shame:
To gain a clear understanding of God's attitude toward sin, we only have to consider the purpose of Christ's death. The

Scripture says, "Without shedding of blood there is no remission" (Hebrews 9:22). There can be no forgiveness of sin unless our debt has been paid. But through the cross, God's love is demonstrated to humanity as he showed us mercy and compassion. Sometimes, when we look out upon the world of nature; water, air, plants and animals, we see the provisions and plans made for our happiness. We discover a revelation of God's love. Yet as wonderful as nature can be in revealing divine love, nothing is comparable to the sacrifice of Calvary. "For God so loved the world that He gave His only begotten Son, that whoever believes in Him should not perish but have everlasting life" (John 3:16).

Grace for a Victorious Future and a destination that is sure:

In the cross we see the way to victory. God makes it plain that our carnal nature was dealt with at the cross, so that in our standing in Christ this nature has no more power over us. We are told that our "old man was crucified with Him" (Romans 6:6) and that we do not need to serve sin any longer. The Scripture promises that sin shall no longer have dominion over us (Romans 6:14). In the cross there is power to overcome Satan and the temptations of life has been given to us. Satan was defeated at the cross.

God's mercy and grace can only be appropriated as we live this experience of the cross daily. This is what Paul meant in Galatians 2:20: "I have been crucified with Christ; it is no longer I who live, but Christ lives in me; and the life which I now live in the flesh I live by faith in the Son of God, who loved me and gave Himself for me." There is no sin that Christ cannot forgive. No struggles and battles that we will face in future that has not already been won. We only need to abide by the power of the cross to give us daily victory. We cannot do it of our won effort. Only God can do it. A victorious daily life is possible. Don't let Satan tell you it is not.

The cross of Christ is not only the basis of our peace and hope–but also the means of our eternal salvation. The goal of the cross is not only a full and free pardon, but a changed life, lived in fellowship with God. Having covered for our sins, Christ presented a glorious future ahead of us not only in eternity but from the moment we believe and are change. Eternal life is not just about Heaven; it starts as soon as you accept Christ. Jesus' purpose was to preach and to heal—and now, so is ours too. The source of His power to do these things was the Holy Spirit, and you have been given the same Holy Spirit that lived in Jesus. This is a major underlying factor and a key winning trick for us. Declare: "In my career, I experience the power of the cross, the power of the Holy Spirit. In my everyday ordinary lives, I experience the power of the cross, I experience the Holy Spirit. In my businesses, I experiences the power of the cross, I experience the Holy Spirit." Keep winning!

Calvary is where God changed everything as the divine exchange occurred. The precious Lamb of God was slain, once and for all. Through this we can enter into the fullness of all God has in store for us. The walls and the barriers were broken down. We now have access to God; the veil has been taken away (Matthew 27:51).

We celebrate the mercy that led to the cleansing of our sins and iniquities. The wages of sin is death. Yet, the resurrection from death and the complete forgiveness for our sins was completed by the work of Christ on Calvary. We celebrate the gift of victory over every fall we have ever experienced, every sorrow we have ever known, every discouragement we have ever had and every fear we have ever faced. The amazing grace of God came and declared us free and fit for a victorious future because of the events that transpired on the cross nearly two millennia ago. As many of us that believe in Christ Jesus, the work of Calvary is being done in us. As the hymn sings:

Mercy there was great, and grace was free;
Pardon there was multiplied to me;
There my burdened soul found liberty,
 At Calvary.

Oh, the love that drew salvation's plan!
Oh, the grace that brought it down to man!
Oh, the mighty gulf that God did span
At Calvary!

His pain on the cross became our gain. That's why the cross is powerful. Jesus Christ suffered, died, and rose from death in order that He could lift us to eternal life. We bear prove of this when we "take up the cross daily" (Luke 9:23), bring flesh and carnal nature to death daily (1 Cor. 15:31) and live our lives in such a way that it is evident that we have "been crucified with Christ and no longer live, but Christ lives in us" (Galatians 2:20). The Calvary road is narrow and could sometimes feel lonely but there is peace, joy, security and abundance. We have the host of heaven and heroes of faith cheering us on.

And can we also add , lastly for the creatives, that Calvary is a place where creativity and vision and ideas that will change our world can be birthed. We can testify that some of our greatest creative businesses venture and most rewarding experiences in life and marriage came from a genuine Calvary experience in our lives. We believe it can be so for you too. Experience the power of the cross today!

Reflection Points:
So the question is, have you visited Calvary today? Are you appropriating the mercy and grace at Calvary to your daily living experience? The Calvary is where the old is

gotten rid of and the new is activated and this can bring a whole new, fresh meaning to life. So go ahead and write down what new thing God is speaking to you about that will impact your world positively. Go through some of the scriptures above again. Experience the power of the cross, experience the Holy Spirit.

Personal Action and Development:

Appropriate the power of the cross over your life today. Decree and declare your victory of sin, shame, regrets and reproach by declaring the power of the cross. Write below and constantly declare to yourself: "I bring my flesh to the Calvary today. I exchange my past and current worries for god's mercy and receive grace for a victorious future.

SOMETIMES, CONFLICT INEVITABLY ARISE AND THOSE ARE CRITICAL TIMES TO SHOW TRUE CHARACTER. OUR ACTIONS AT THESE SENSITIVE MOMENTS CAN EITHER INSPIRE OR DEMORALIZE FOLLOWERS, ONLOOKERS OR OBSERVERS.

When there is conflict, speak softly (Proverbs 15:1), be honest (Romans 12:17) and work toward peace as a Child of God. Think of Love, good reports and virtue (Philippians 4:8). In Matthew 18:15 we are reminded that "…if your brother sins against you, go and tell him his fault between you and him alone. If he hears you, you have gained your brother."

HOW WE MANAGE CONFLICT TELLS WHO WE TRULY ARE

Conflict will always arise in life as we deal with people from different walks of life. If you're human, you have probably experienced conflict or betrayal. You can add disappointments and stress to the list. We're all in some sort of relationship with someone – some of them could be difficult and they could include our peers, direct reports, managers, family members and even close friends. Communication exchange can easily escalate when the other person involved also reacts without thinking first, turning a conversation into a heated argument or leading to passive-aggressive behavior like backstabbing or gossiping.

Whether you recognize yourself as a leader or not, you are influencing someone in one way or the other. We have stressed this in this book already that you are a leader in one form or another; in what you do and in the little roles you play. **Therefore when conflict arises, we must work very hard not to react on the spot. We must not be impulsive or short-sighted.** We need to handle tough situations skillfully so that it will not boil down to a level that we lose it and make people around us uncomfortable.

By responding, rather than reacting, Marcel Schwantes (Principal and founder, *Leadership From the Core*) retorts that we create space to consider the situation and decide the best approach to handle things. He further identified responding to include three main things:

Patience: We use this leadership virtue to our advantage to assess a situation, get perspective, listen without judgment, process, and hold back from reacting head on. It's the decision to sit on your decision. By thinking it over rationally, you'll eventually arrive at other, more sane conclusions. While patience may be bitter, its fruit is oh-so-sweet.

Humility: We avoid the temptation of reacting from our bruised egos with a sarcastic comeback, put down, or stomping on the warpath for revenge. We draw instead from our inner strength, trusting in the moment to a different, better, outcome.

Self-Awareness: We look at the whole picture and both sides of the issue. We tap into our feelings and those of others to choose a different outcome, like a compassionate response to solving an interpersonal problem.

Daniel Goleman, the emotional intelligence guru, says: "If your emotional abilities aren't in hand, if you don't have self-awareness, if you are not able to manage your distressing emotions, if you can't have empathy and have effective relationships, then no matter how smart you are, you are not going to get very far."

Diffusing Conflict with a compassionate response is the way to go. The next time someone flies off the handle on you, here's a way to positively blow that person away with your response. Try asking, "Are you OK? What's going on?" Then…just…listen. What will follow may surprise you. You will most likely open up the door for the other person to explain the issue behind the issue. Now you have arrived at another great opportunity: to diffuse a situation through open discourse.

While this, like other ideas we shared in this book may be difficult to develop and practice, especially when it involves a remarkably difficult person, making the effort over time will lead to a positive outcome not only for you but people who are within our immediate environment and sphere of influence. This is another example of the paradigm shift we want this book to establish in our readers.

Reflection Points:

How do you manage conflicts? Do you usually go head on with the other counterparty or do you hold back and not respond until you have a better way to handle the situation. It is going to be undoubtedly hard to hold back but it comes with practice, personal awareness and discipline. As we discussed in previous sections, we can help those along our sphere of influence to learn valuable life lessons by holding back our negative reaction and responding with grace.

Personal Action and Development:

Do you have a current conflict situation? Based on the above discussion, list out steps on how you will handle conflict and the potential benefits that can be derived from doing so. Make effort to meditate on the benefits you listed. You can use a post-it note to stick it somewhere to remind you when a sudden conflicting situation arise. This tip might be especially useful for those who are in a current tough situation.

DREAM BIG. YOU ARE A DIVINE ORIGINAL AND THE WORLD NEEDS YOUR UNIQUE CONTRIBUTION.

"For You formed my inward parts; You wove me in my mother's womb. I will give thanks to You, for I am fearfully and wonderfully made; Wonderful are Your works, And my soul knows it very well." (Psalm 139:19-14). "I knew you before I formed you in your mother's womb. Before you were born I set you apart and appointed you as my prophet to the nations." (Jeremiah 1:5 NLT)

DREAM BIG, YOU ARE A DIVINE ORIGINAL

There is no other person like you in the whole universe. Take a moment to let that sink in. You are a divine original. **That there is no other person like you, out of the 7.2 billion people all over the world, should make you feel very excited yet humbled.** Renowned fingerprint scientist Sir Francis Galton calculated the probability of two whole fingerprints matching and found the result to be somewhere around one in 64 billion (1.5625e-13%) — making your fingerprints uniquely yours out of the 7.2 billion people around the world. Your iris (eyes), tongue, gait and ears are unique. And as unique as you are, God knows you to every detail. That's deep isn't it? Isaiah 43:1 indicates that God knows us all by name. God knows us at the genetic level – the level of our DNA.

In Luke 12:7, Jesus talks to His followers about how much personal interest God takes in them. The detail he mentions is that "the very hairs of your head are all numbered." The creative abilities of Eugene H. Peterson makes this point more beautiful in The Message Translation of Psalm 139:14-16: "Body and soul, I am marvelously made! Bit by bit, how I was sculpted from nothing into something" Each of us has been carefully modeled and designed to provide a unique contribution. You are a divine original. So next time you look in the mirror, remember that there is no other person who looks exactly like you.

That you are unique then means your life cannot be a waste, it cannot be useless. That you are absolutely distinct then brings on some sense responsibility to fulfill your unique role on earth. There is no other version of you. God has specifically created you to fulfill a purpose here on earth. Understanding this is a fundamental key to success.

The situation that has become very prevalent is that rather than focus on their divine originality, a lot of people spend time copying another person. This inadvertently make people that copy look like fakes in the end. As we mentioned in the "You Have A Divine Pathway Section", to make unique contribution that is as authentic as our DNA, we require we live our lives as originally as we can.

Originality can be cultivated. There is the widespread assumption that nothing is new under the sun and that it's ok to copy. Our personal recommendation is to avoid mindless copying. If you practice the power of solitude consistently, you will have access to great untapped creative energy/creativity that is yet to be revealed to the world. If you see a great idea that you feel the urge to copy, convert the urge to a creative process of understanding how that idea came to being. You can use the distillation method (recommended in the "Power of Solitude" sections in this book) to break components apart and attempt to re-engineer. After the re-engineering process is complete and your final outcome still doesn't feel or look original, you may want to consider doing further re-engineering.

Dream big and be determined to be original. By so doing you provide your own unique contribution to the world and other people's lives. Dream big. Be original. You further inspire and encourage people who are committed to being originals including ourselves. By doing this, you enlist yourself as champions of the new paradigm for originality.

But what if your original idea appear to have been stolen or copied by someone else even before it reaches day light? Here is what we recommend in such a case: do a benefit-cost analysis. Does the cost of chasing down the thief outweigh the benefit? If it is too costly we recommend you leave it. Most times, when we go back and ask God for fresh ideas, He always gives new inspiration for producing something better. God is the source of creativity and originality. Those of us who are close to the heart of God enjoy the privilege of fresh ideas, clarity of vision and unlimited access to originality.

Working on this Live Love Learn Grow project brought new meaning and depth to us about originality. Each graphic art (especially in the coffee table edition), the reflection points and personal action and development (PADs) concepts, the accompanying T-Shirts and the quote picture frames are all products of original thoughts and ideas. This project has further strengthened our resolve for authenticity. We have also come to know how to identify individuals who pursue originality and to celebrate them. Originality requires some effort. Copying is cheap. **Pursuing originality enlarges dreams and vision. Copying makes us small and myopic in nature.**

Reflection points:
Do you regard yourself as a divine original or are you feeling like a fake or counterfeit? Could it be that you lack originality because you have been mindlessly copying other people's work or lifestyle instead of looking unto the ultimate source - God - for divine inspiration? In what way do you think you can experience originality and authenticity in your life? What steps or change do you need to make to experience a new reality and vitality? Do you agree that the environment you are goes a long way in influencing how you think, act and embrace originality?

Personal Action and Development:
Being original take some little effort but with time it becomes a lifestyle. Resist the urge to copy. You can tap inspiration from others but avoid copying their works or even themselves. Attempt to decompose and re-engineer an idea. Work towards building your own prototype, a new product or service. From today, make the tangible effort to reference, give credit or mention to who is due. Make a list of people who are committed to originality in their

endeavours: artist, business men developing new models or solutions/approach, song writers, composers, designers, etc. Encourage them in whatever way you feel to. You can give us a shout on social media when you get here to encourage us too for this original book you are reading. We will truly appreciate it! :)

INTEGRITY ELEVATES OUR PERSONAL, BUSINESS OR ORGANIZATION'S BRANDS TO A HIGHER LEVEL. ALTHOUGH HARD TO CULTIVATE, IT SERVES AS THE BADGE FOR LONG-TERM SUCCESS.

"But let your communication be, Yea, yea; Nay, nay: for whatsoever is more than these cometh of evil."
Matthew 5:37

INTEGRITY: THE BADGE FOR LONG-TERM SUCCESS

True, integrity is about moral uprightness and honesty. More than just a mere term however, integrity should be seen as a holistic concept either personally or across our entire businesses (small, large, medium, public, private, government and not-for-profit). We tend to only focus on the outward part of integrity where we spend so much money and time in order to maintain consistent approach to facilities, decor, colour, dress and branding. Yet it goes beyond what can readily be seen. **As individuals, we must develop a process of internalizing integrity. We need to ensure that we speak from the core of our hearts and follow through with whatever promise or commitments we have given.** Across the organization, integrating both internal (operational) and external (customer facing) components of our businesses is the number one sure sign of success. In other words, brands (personal and corporate) must always demonstrate a level of internal and external consistency that is characteristic of strong, trustworthy identity and personality.

Integrity is making our values, goals, words and priorities align so that our message stays consistent and not mixed. Integrity is having the resolve to make our personal and business pursuit value oriented rather than money oriented. This isn't easy, but brands that follow through usually succeed. Success without integrity really isn't true or sustainable success at all. Integrity is long-term and those taking shortcuts, cutting corners and bending rules can't make it long term.

Note however that this does not mean you don't save time by doing things quicker and being more efficient with time and available resources. We are aware of the school of thoughts that alludes to breaking the rules as a way of innovating disruptively. But that is not what we are addressing in this context. We are not saying that you don't' save time by doing things quicker. **Being a person or business of integrity doesn't mean you have to be slow.** What we are saying is this: integrity is making it a top priority to leave lasting impressions in the heart of people or customers by doing the right thing – and doing the right thing innovatively and quicker sounds even more terrific. What we are primarily emphasizing is to make integrity a top priority – do what you promise, let it come from your heart, leave lasting impressions. **Integrity is a key component of good personal or business character formation and together with other noble qualities, it fortifies and beautifies true brand identity.**

People will remember you most, not for what you say or the colour of your dress but by how you treat them. And how you treat people is a function of the integrity you carry inside of you. Those with integrity keep their words, even when it hurts. Integrity is making values-based decisions, not decisions based on personal gains or self-gratification. **No one is perfect, we all make mistakes, but those with integrity admit their mistakes and do what they can to right the wrong.**

Leaders with integrity are more concerned about their character than their reputation. Your reputation is merely who others think you are, but your character is who you really are. This therefore makes integrity of paramount importance for good leadership – it's a given.

In making promises and declaring our intents, Jesus advises, "let your communication be, Yea, yea; Nay, nay" (Matthew 5:37 KJV). By doing this our integrity is built and solidified. We do what is right before men and God (John 14:6). Ultimately, through our integrity, God will uphold us (Psalm 41:12).

As we wrap up this section, we want you to always keep in mind that with integrity, influence is sustained, power maintained and trust obtained. It is the hallmark of truly legendary personal and business brands.

Reflection Points:

Have you been confronted with a situation where what you said was false or your presentation has false information? How did you handle the accusation? Those moments can help build our integrity as we respond with sincerity and honesty, admitting our wrongs and making amends. Integrity is communicating truthfulness from our heart. We allow what we say to be truthful and valid. People can trust us and believe in us. It is not that things will not change but prior to and during change, we can communicate effectively with stakeholders as a means of upholding ethos of integrity.

Come to think of it, integrity is hard to build and can easily be crushed. But we can rebuild it again by starting today. Clear yourself of falsehood. The way you present yourself and your conduct. Let everything align to your true and honest purpose from the heart. Observe how your integrity grows.

Personal Action and Development:

List a few ways you personally feel your uprightness, honesty and values can help build your integrity. For example you may want to write that: "Because I am a Christian, I will ensure that I do not lie or cheat in my business conduct and motive no matter how much money I would have made" I promise not to be fraudulent in my day to day personal and business transactions" Go ahead and write your personal statements of integrity below.

IT IS BECOMING INCREASINGLY OBVIOUS THAT IT IS THOSE THAT DARE TO DO THE IMPOSSIBLE THAT ACTUALLY ACCOMPLISH SOMETHING GREAT IN THEIR LIFETIME.

"That is what the Scriptures mean when they say, "No eye has seen, no ear has heard, and no mind has imagined what God has prepared for those who love him." 1 Corinthians 2:9

DARE THE IMPOSSIBLE

People that dare the impossible are the ones that actually change our world. There are a number of stories we can learn from on the topic of daring the impossible but the story of the bridge between Manhattan and Brooklyn stands out.

When John Roebling devised a plan to build a bridge between Manhattan and Brooklyn in 1869, experts of that time said it was "impossible". John Roebling however died in the course of the construction due to an accident that occurred while conducting surveys for the bridge project. But that didn't stop the project. His son, Washington, took over the project. Not long after, Washington too had an accident and got brain damaged – unable to talk or walk. It was Washington's wife, Emily Warren Roebling, who had taken it upon herself to learn bridge construction, became his nurse, companion, and confidant and took over much of the chief engineer's duties including day-to-day supervision and project management. Washington had developed a special way of communicating with his wife while he was incapacitated. Despite the challenges that confronted them, in 1883, the Brooklyn Bridge was completed – 14years after it was originally started.

When Larry Page and Sergy Brin decided to download the whole web on to their computer, people thought they were crazy. That they accomplished it was how Google started in the 90s. Page said they had a "healthy disregard for the impossible."

When we decided to start providing scholarship grants to students in Africa through OyES Education, people we shared the vision with thought it was impossible. Others gave us many other reasons why it shouldn't be done. They were looking at our current situations. Coming from non-wealthy homes, with little to nothing from personal savings and student allowance, it actually looked like it was not going to be possible. But we had a strong determination to help African youths who wanted to go to school and didn't have the financial means to. We managed to put all our efforts together and OyES scholarship kicked off in 2013. It still continues annually till date, providing scholarship and ongoing academic support to university students.

Most times we allow the voices of mediocre and lacklustre people swallow up our courage. Sometimes, it is our own inner fear (of failure) that kill our determination and resolve. So we set the small "possible" limits of what we can do or accomplish. Where did we put our faith to do the extraordinary? What happened to the clear statement in John 14:12 that "greater things you will do"? What about 2Timothy 1:7 stating clearly that we have the spirit that empowers us and gives us sound minds (to see the invisible)? And what about the declaration that the eyes of the world have not yet seen what great things are in store (1Corinthians 2:9)? **How about if we launch for something greater, be focused and determined to do what average people call "impossible"?** How powerful could it be to extend our vision, scope and mindset to new "impossible" levels of doing what God has called us to do?

Yes, it will sound crazy to even yourself and maybe you have a feeling you may not accomplish a BIG vision. But if you work towards it, you will realize you ultimately grow into new levels. Just the opportunity to dream and envision new possibilities is empowering on its own. We can raise the limits and set new personal best for ourselves. Daring the impossible also allows us tap new energy, new inspiration and clarify our God-given vision as we raise the bar Higher.

Ok, so you decided to dare the impossible but where do I start you ask? Tell yourself: I can do it with the help of

God! Speak to yourself from your heart. **When you want something to show up in your outward man, deposit God's Word in the inward man.** The time is now. Dare the impossible!

Reflection points

Picking off from your last major accomplishment, set a BIG (a little crazy) target for your next accomplishment. Yes, write it down. You may refer back to some of our previous notes to help fine tune your vision e.g. "Power of Solitude". See also Appendix 7 in operating from your core; the blessed, empowered and divine you that God has made.

Then take a look at what you wrote down. Begin to take action. Take baby (growth) steps and begin to work towards it. It may look overwhelming but as you begin to decompose the compounds to molecules and to atomic units you will get to the nucleus of that great idea. Watch as your passion to do something begins to motivate people to join you and God begins to raise people to work collaboratively with you in accomplishing the "Impossible" because of your faith. Keep moving little by little. You are on your way to accomplishing the impossible.

Personal Action and Development:

What is the biggest thing you ever dream of in your life? No matter how big it is, we want you to know that it is achievable. Write it below in bold letters and put in front of it "ACCOMPLISHED". Take a step back and draw a plan that will help you grow to achieve it in a sustainable way (remember it is not just goals but also growth).

AN INDIVIDUAL THAT HAS DEVELOPED A CONTINUOUS VALUE-ADDING LIFESTYLE USUALLY BRINGS VALUE TO THE ENVIRONMENT THEY OPERATE. VALUE-ORIENTED INDIVIDUALS ARE OUTSTANDING ASSETS TO ANY INSTITUTION.

In Mark 3:14 we read: "And he ordained twelve, that they should be with him, and that he might send them forth to preach". In 1 Kings 6:7 it was stated that "The stones used in the construction of the Temple were finished at the quarry, so there was no sound of hammer, ax, or any other iron tool at the building site." Denying ourselves, taking up the cross, furnishing and building ourselves at the quarry and being with Jesus are value adding process that makes us outstanding individuals and excellent team members.

BECOME A VALUE-ORIENTED INDIVIDUAL

Great players are those that have been trained, furnished and grown into champions. **We call this process of furnishing, training and equipping the value adding process.** Having a value orientation is important because we have seen very sincere, honest and hardworking people who have clear intentions to contribute but lack substance and therefore couldn't bring any significant value to the group or system.

It is important to also mention that value orientation can be viewed from two perspectives: value as intrinsic, invisible qualities we carry within us and value as tangible goods and service produced. We used the two interchangeably in this section as we discuss value.

We are seeing more and more that it is men and women who are seasoned - champions - that can bring about lasting positive change in our society. We are talking about men and women of value whose way of life have been shaped by firm belief and faith. Men and women that have their core principles in things that not only yield material or financial rewards but also things that are morally upright, intangible, **unbusinesslike** benefits to humanity. It is rather unfortunate that we have individuals who want to make significant change in the society but lack any value proposition neither have they added value to themselves. We hold this resolve that it is individual that have developed a continuous value adding lifestyle that usually bring value to the environment they operate. Value-oriented individuals are outstanding assets to any church, organization or institution. So we strongly encourage you to become one yourself. Make value adding your lifestyle. Become value oriented.

So how do I become a value-oriented individual you ask? We can pick cues from the scripture. Jesus used this value adding method in building the legendary team of disciples that ultimately spread the gospel making it far reaching even to people like myself and you thousands of years later. In Mark 3:14 we read: "And he ordained twelve, **that they should be with him**, and that he might send them forth to preach". In 1 Kings 6:7 scriptures says " The stones used in the construction of the Temple were **prefinished** at the quarry, so the entire structure was built without the sound of hammer, ax, or any other tool at the building site." See, when we take the time and effort to be built, nurtured, taught, equipped in the proper way, it makes our manifestation look effortless. Part of our reasoning is that when there is noise, conflict or discord within a group or system (i.e. the temple, the house, etc.), it could be an indication of poorly built individuals or leaders.

Denying ourselves, taking up the cross, furnishing and building ourselves at the quarry (daily Calvary experience if you connect the dots back to previous sections) and being with Jesus are value adding process that makes us outstanding individuals and excellent team members. The quarry is a dirty place. Messy and rough. We can chisel and hammer out irrelevances and build on our core competency. Quarry is where no one will appreciate what we look like. But when we come out of the quarry, we look golden, beautiful and complete. We also seamlessly become compatible with other quality people who have added value to themselves in the same way. This is so because people that know their worth, have identified that unique area of calling and are operating within a divine pathway have the natural tendency to identify and work with people who are doing the same.

It is important to know yourself and where you are in the value scale (self-awareness). Knowing where you are will help you know how much time you need to spend building yourself first. Spend time at the "quarry", then go ahead and start adding value to people around you. Be a blessing to them. Serve others. Try lots of different things. Solve people's problems. Don't focus on money, focus on value creation. You will gain more as you continue to accumulate value in yourself.

But it all starts with a thought process which produces spirit-filled manifestations. Philippians 4:8 says: "whatsoever things are true, whatsoever things are honest, whatsoever things are just, whatsoever things are pure, whatsoever things are lovely, whatsoever things are of good report; if there be any virtue, and if there be any praise, think on these things." Think. Think about a quality life. Think about excellence. Here are some of the ingredients in the lives of value-oriented individuals (intrinsic): good communication, patience, long-suffering, courage, endurance, faith, discipline, determination, dedication and focus. Some of the qualities we have also mentioned in various sections of this book qualify as value add (e.g. embracing diversity, building team working skills, etc). These are qualities to add along the value adding wheel.

What we have found very fascinating is that while the workplace environment and business landscape continue to change, value oriented individuals will continue to stand and remain highly sort after. This is what we have found to be our personal testimonies. So we encourage you to be value oriented.

Continue to find meaning and essence in your daily living as you add value to yourself. As you continue to know yourself through on going self-awareness and evaluation, you develop strengths of Character (honesty, integrity, perseverance and strong work ethics) which will help you withstand the test of time. Be open to positive criticism and explore new opportunities. Keep a learning attitude and keep adding value to yourself continuously. The journey is both a revelation (from God) and a discovery (for you). Along the journey, you will find connection with your core values and purpose in life. As you continue to move forward in a value oriented way, you will develop strong spiritual senses and become clearer in vision and purpose. It is the value you carry that connects and resonates with like-minded people. God will be placing people around you that you can grow and advance together. Live a life of value!

Reflection points:

Do a self-evaluation. Do you appreciate the need to add value to yourself? When last did you help solve other people's problems? When last did you create value (intrinsic or tangible)?

Personal Action and Development:

So start today. Start now. Start from the small things and move to greater things. We developed a value adding loop which shown in Appendix 1. You can also download an image of the value adding loop here: http://oyeseducation.org/wp-content/uploads/2017/02/Value-Adding-Loop.png.
There are more resources to study on value orientation including an introductory video on the resource section of the oyeseducation.org website.

We want to close with this personal development question: who are those that you can reach out to today that will help you maintain a value adding lifestyle? List those people and reach out to them about adding more value to yourself.

VISIONARIES USUALLY BECOME LEADERS BECAUSE VISION IMPOSES A CERTAIN DISCIPLINE AND FOCUS THAT CRYSTALLIZES IN THE EXCELLENCE WE ALL ADMIRE. SHOW ME A PERSON OF VISION AND I WILL SHOW YOU SOMEONE DESTINED FOR GREATNESS.

Get A vision for your life. Ask for it. God will show you. In Jeremiah 33:3 (MSG) we read: 'Call to me and I will answer you. I'll tell you marvelous and wondrous things that you could never figure out on your own.' Habakkuk 2:2 (KJV) says: "And the LORD answered me, and said, Write the vision, and make it plain upon tables, that he may run that readeth it."

BECOME VISION ORIENTED

Vision is so important in life! Vision is the ability to see through the invisible, intangible and inconsequential things to create something of value and significance. What differentiates an ordinary person from an extraordinary one is the quality of their vision.

First off, Vision is not formed by just being futuristic. We are talking of vision that produces a mission; vision that is actionable and propels you to work. You see, vision is not just day dreaming and making white-washed declarations as we see many do. Vision is not made up of only the present information either. Our past also add shades of colour to what we see. Vision is having a clear grasp of where we are coming from, where we are at the moment and projecting into the future.

Also, when we are talking about vision in this book, we are not referring to the boring, corporate terminologies and bureaucratic mambo jumbo that appears to be monotonous and of little effect in driving any significant change. **We are referring to vision here as a clear future-focused big picture specific enough to shape decision-making and appropriately broad to allow innovative strategies for realizing the vision.** We see vision as relevant to time and context, value-based, purposeful and unique. Well-articulated vision should invite both ourselves and our organizations to greatness. Vision represents a future beyond what is possible today or what we think possible tomorrow. Vision is an invitation to a tomorrow or destination of greatness. It is the highest level goal that should challenge us if viewed on an individual basis or the institutions we represent if viewed from a corporate point of view. Vision helps us to see into a future better than today thereby elevating our hopes and aspirations. Vision is really crucial in our lives as individuals or as an institution.

Vision clarifies and qualifies purpose and gives us direction in life. When an individual has a vision for his or her life, there is the tendency to move in a direction that will make the vision clearer and achievable. This so happens because people with vision (visionaries) tend to attract the right people and resources. Vision attracts resources. Vision comes with **expansionary** and **constrictionary** properties as well.

Expansionary: vision allows us to see, operate and live beyond what we physically have (our assets) – launching us into the realm of trading in invisible, intangible things supernaturally secured by God. In effect, vision has the capacity to attract resources.

Conversely, vision also comes with **constriction** consequences that we need to keep in mind as we desire a clearer vision, meaning and purpose for our lives. Vision pre-imposes focus and discipline. It tends to narrow down your capabilities into purposeful, result oriented action items. The implication of this is that you tend to loose connection with things that are not in line with your purpose. This sometimes include apparent friends, relations or associates who have no role to play in your future nor in helping you in fulfilling your God-given vision. Vision makes you very disciplined and focused. Vision is such that when you walk in line with it, people that are not going to collaborate or help you get it accomplished usually don't feature in it. It is sad that this also happens to be our close friends and family sometimes – people that God has not placed to be relevant in our purpose and will not feature in the fulfilment of our God-given vision.

So how do you catch a vision? There is really no straight answer to this. We will however try our best to explain from our personal experience and see if it can help you get started. See, we are all different. Our visions are different but they carry similar characteristics. The characteristics and qualities of what we see are incumbent on our past and our present. So as you read this, take a moment to think. Dream again. What has been your previous experience (good or bad)? What have you learnt from them? What are you projecting into the future with your experiences and what are your personal growth projections going forward. Chances are that the opportunities and privileges you have been exposed to and the challenges and victories you have witnessed are pointing towards a destination. You just have to see it.

Vision encompasses many pieces of information of who we are; whether we are looking at the subject from a personal or business point of view. We can catch a vision by gathering key information. Vision therefore becomes a perfect blend of information relating to our past, history, current realities, culture, experiences, values, goals, ideas, and desired future. The place of solitude help refine and clarify vision as you carefully process these information. Let's give a personal example.

That I (Oluwaseun) was born in a military-led government era in Nigeria where leadership and accountability became very crucial gave me a strong reason to want to learn and understand the dynamics of good leadership. Having come from that background, looking at where I am today and what I see in future, my vision is for GOOD leadership qualities to be visible and accessible. That connects ultimately with raising a generation of young people from early age. Part of what I see myself doing is laying the correct foundation for sound personal/individual principles on which good leadership can be built. For someone else (as another example), vision would be to have been born in poverty, got help and broke out of that poverty, acquired enough wealth to project a vision of ending poverty. Your vision is unique. It contains a past and a present that you can project into the future.

Sometimes, what we refer to as vision could actually be a process we call **RE-vision**. RE-vision is a process of fine-tuning our original vision as we grow in knowledge and wisdom and God releases or exposes us to more information relevant to shape what we see.

So once the thinking process starts, begin to write things out. Keep in mind that all that God will have you become as a person – your purpose, like a seed - is already in you (See Appendix 7). Start by looking from within you not from the outside. Write from your heart.

Write out your vision by first writing all the desires of your heart (no matter how many they are or the number of pages they contain. By now, we hope you have already gotten an idea pad or personal reflection journal where you have included thoughts, action items and plans from previous sections. If you haven't done so before, now is a perfect time to do so). Second, simplify all that you have written into simple multiple sentences. It is ok if it still looks like a lot. Ensure to document this steps. Again an idea pad or journal will be relevant here. If necessary do another Re-vision as explained above.

Finally narrow the multiple sentences into one sentence that is inspirational, emotional and can be effectively communicated. Map out a plan around your vision and take action in the direction of your vision. Do more RE-vision momentarily.

What you will realize as you live with vision, purpose and intentionality is that you are gradually physically moving in directions that is growth oriented, purposeful and authentic. You become easy to follow because you are walking in line with a precise line of calling upon your life. People that truly change and impact our world are people with vision.

Thank God for the internet and all the great things we can do with it. But as powerful as these technologies can be, they cannot change the world. It is men and women with dreams, visions and ideas behind these systems that cause change to occur. Its men and women of dreams and vision who have taken action that cause change to occur in our world. They inspire others, are a blessing to the society and cause lasting positive change to take place.

Dream big. Let your vision inspire other people. Let it appeal to hearts and minds. Let it be uplifting.

Reflection Point:

Do you have a vision? Do you need a RE-vision? Are you just only seeing things and not writing it down? Because you are working in line with your vision, what expansionary and contractionary trade-offs are you experiencing? Do you agree that what you are born to do is so much bigger than what you are doing right now? Can you see a vision of the big picture?

Personal Action and Development:

If you haven't done so yet, catch a vision for a purposeful life today. Visions don't have to be caught while sleeping or in a dream. Vision can be derived while we are wide awake, even in the middle of a task. But RE-vision helps you fine-tune it and to help you put it all together in such a way that it can be communicated. So grab your writing pad or journal and start with the first step of writing the desires, ideas and purposes of your heart no matter how many they are. We have a number of resources on vision, purpose and mission at www.oyeseducation.org/resources. You can access these as further personal action and development tools.

MINDSET PREDETERMINES A NUMBER OF THINGS ESPECIALLY: CHARACTER FORMATION, LEARNING OUTCOMES AND WHETHER OR NOT WE SEE OURSELVES IN THE LIGHT OF OUR TRUE POTENTIAL.

The state of our mind determines whether we see a battle ahead and declare victory or call ourselves "grasshoppers" (Numbers 13:33). Our mindset will also determine whether we stay hopeless or take calculated faith-guided risks as in the case of the four lepers (2 Kings 7:3-13). The state of our mind will determine whether we settle and eat the king's food or stay without food and glorify God (Daniel 1:8).

A GOOD MINDSET

Mindset, according to Collins English dictionary are the ideas and attitudes with which a person approaches a situation, especially when these are seen as being difficult to alter. It can also be regarded as a fixed mental attitude or disposition that predetermines a person's responses to and interpretations of situations. The American Heritage® Stedman's Medical Dictionary refer to mindset as: "An inclination or a habit". These habits eventually become our character. Our inclinations, attitudes and interpretation to difficult situations determine whether we see it as a learning opportunity or as a dead end. **That we consistently live in light of our true potential or operate as though we are inadequate or unequal to the task is a function of our mental predisposition – mindset.** So mindset is key and of high importance.

We felt it would be good to start by providing an understanding of the mind and how it works. The mind is between our soul and spirit. No one can actually say specifically where it is located. Scripture also use the heart and mind interchangeably (Hebrews 8:10, 1 Samuel 2:35, Psalm 26:2). Researches are yet to determine its actual location. Some conclude that it is nowhere. But one thing we certainly know about the mind is that it is the storehouse of information that we receive. It also serves as a processing centre. For example, a mind that has consistently been exposed to violence and indiscriminate use of guns or other weapons can only process to shoot whenever he/she sees a gun. **It is the preconditioning by exposure to information that makes the mind very unique.**

A child is born innocent but as time goes by, the information the baby is exposed to, whether negative or positive, preconditions the child's mind. Based on these sets of information, a specific pattern of knowledge is built. It therefore follows that for every action or impact we experience, the mind processes those signals and responds or reacts based on pre-formed knowledge already coded into the mind. Sadly, our minds have been corrupted by the world so we need to make the effort to renew it. Scripture says: "Do not be conformed to the world, but be transformed by the renewing of your mind" (Romans 12:2).

The story in Numbers 13 and 14 captures how important our state of mind can be. God had already promised the children of Israel that He was going to take them to the promised land of Canaan "flowing with milk and honey" (Exodus 3:8). A certain group containing twelve leaders were later required to go spy the Promised Land. The group came back with two reports about the land. Ten of them came back with a negative report while two of them – Caleb and Joshua - came back with a positive report. **Same situation, two reports. The diverging point: their mindsets**.

Both parties apparently agree "It truly flows with milk and honey, and this is its fruit" (Numbers 13:27) but they diverged in their ability to receive the promise that it belongs to them because of the difficult situation they perceived on the land. The naysayers insist in their report: "the people who dwell in the land are strong; the cities are fortified and very large... they are stronger than we... we were like grasshoppers in our own sight, and so we were in their sight" (Numbers 13:31-33). Caleb retorted: "Let's go up and take control, because we can definitely conquer it." (Numbers 13:30) Joshua further added: "If the Lord delights in us, then He will bring us into this land and give it to us." (Numbers 14: 8)

Majority, as they say, wins the vote and as a result, the Israelites stayed another 37 years in the desert before entering the Promised Land. **Mindset is a determining**

factor. If we have a mind filled with faith and not fear, that we can enter into the fullness of God's provisions of grace, we will. Joshua and Caleb illustrated this truth by entering the Promised Land despite the naysayers and all the odds.

The lepers in 2 Kings 7:3-13 thought to themselves, "Why sit we here until we die?" They were using their minds – processing information and signals. They were reasoning. God said, "Come now, and let us reason together, saith the Lord…" (Isaiah 1:8). The Hebrew word translated "reason" means "argue, convince". In other words, think it over. Look at all sides of the question until you are convinced. Get the right mindset. So the lepers rose up in the twilight and went into the camp and behold, there was no man there. But there was food to keep them alive. They came to the uttermost part of the camp, they went into one tent, and did eat and drink, and carried thence silver, and gold, and raiment…" (2 Kings 7:8)

Daniel and his three friends were determined and purposed in their mind not to eat the food. The result: they looked healthier (Daniel 1:15). Not surprised to see the outstanding result this type of mindset produced in them. Scriptures recorded: " In every matter of wisdom and understanding about which the king questioned them, he found them ten times better than all the magicians and enchanters in his whole kingdom.." (Daniel 1:20 NIV).

Our mindsets are shaped by what we take in. If we continue to accept God's positive report for our lives we develop good habits which are the bedrock for good character. Good character and attitude can carry us through tough situations as we turn on a learning perspective instead of a "loosing" perspective. **We operate in the light of our true potential, with vision and purpose when we have a good mindset.**

We encourage you to have a mindset that is fixed on God and that produces godly, positive values. Don't have a fixed mindset that limits your horizon and potentiality. We encourage you to have a growth-oriented mindset. Be courageous and purposeful. Don't be afraid or timid. Be committed to seeing things through the eyes of faith as you allow God use situations to shape and strengthen your character. You are empowered. You are equipped. You only need the right mindset to see it. You can reach your full potential in life, businesses and career with the right mindset.

Reflection Points:

What is the state of your mind? Like the pessimistic 10 or the optimistic 2 our mindset will determine how we view things? Where do you feel you need a change of habit or attitude so that you can develop a good character? Is your mind feeling week and lost? Are you confused and almost sundering to difficult circumstances? Maybe it's time to renew your mind and not be conformed to situations and circumstances trying to hold you down. Do not be conformed, but be transformed by the renewing of your mind (Romans 12:2).

Personal Action And Development:

It just takes small little changes doesn't it? To change a bad habit to a good one and ultimately develop a good character, you only require to have the right mindset. After identifying habits that need to change, plan a way to change it. We strongly recommend feeding more on the word of God and hanging around great people who appear to have a positive appearance to life and potentially good mindset.

HUMILITY AND A HEART OF SERVICE HAVE SOMETHINIG TO DO WITH GREATNESS.

"Jesus called them together and said, "You know that the rulers of the Gentiles lord it over them, and their high officials exercise authority over them. Not so with you. Instead, whoever wants to become great among you must be your servant, and whoever wants to be first must be your slave— just as the Son of Man did not come to be served, but to serve, and to give his life as a ransom for many."" Matthew 20:25-28 (NIV)

TRUE GREATNESS – IT GOES BEYOND MERE SUCCESS

Let's take a moment to look at greatness and success from a deeper perspective. **That a friend be willing to lay down his life for another is greatness.** That we live for a purpose over and beyond mere success is greatness. That we give something that caters to the inner being more than outward adornment is greatness. That we serve each other is greatness. That we are humble is greatness. These definitions for greatness are not the contemporary type we know of.

The issue of being great has always crossed my mind just as it does the mind of every single one of us. We all want to be great. And it didn't start with us. The very issue of greatness can be traced back to the disciples while they were with Jesus. Their minds were constantly asking: who will be the first, who will be the head or most significant or highly recognized among the group. The topic was such an important matter that the mother of two of the disciples, James and John, brought her two sons forth as candidates for greatness. She came with a single request: "grant that one of these two sons of mine may sit at your right and the other at your left in your kingdom" (Matthew 20:21). She was sincere and honest about the question and wanted her Children to be exceedingly great. After all, she knows this very Jesus; the very chosen of God - the messiah – had the ability to make her children great. She is a fantastic mother, looking out for her Children and insisting that they must be in a good place.

The reaction of the remaining ten disciples actually shows that they were all having the same longing. They have all been nursing the feeling of being like the master Jesus. "When the ten heard about this, they were indignant with the two brothers" (Matthew 20:24). They felt even more displeased that James and John had to bring their mother into a matter they have all been arguing about. See, everyone wants to be great. And we see this trend in every walks of life from politics to teaching and clergy. We all aim to be at the top and want to be the leader in front, leading the pack. The more common term used today is to be the "boss", commanding and controlling others. But it was Jesus' response to the matter of greatness that sets the backdrop upon which we attempt to build the points in this section. Jesus' response brought in a totally new paradigm to the issue of greatness, success and leadership.

"Jesus called them together and said, "You know that the rulers of the Gentiles lord it over them, and their high officials exercise authority over them. Not so with you. Instead, whoever wants to become great among you must be your servant, and whoever wants to be first must be your slave— just as the Son of Man did not come to be served, but to serve, and to give his life as a ransom for many." Matthew 20:25-28 (NIV).

Therein lays the principle of servant leadership that has become so scarce in our modern time. This very scripture brought a whole new perspective into our understanding of greatness. It is not the BIG success that the world claims it to be. It is not "lording" over people or just exercising authority. There appears to be more to it. Some peoples' entire lives are dedicated to being just successful in gathering money and material stuff. It makes sense to do that. Material success is extremely important in life. Individually and collectively as a couple, we have experienced success and know what it means. But more than being "successful", living significantly and leaving positive, lasting legacy in the life of others is more important. That is true greatness. **You see, humility and a heart of Service have something to do with true GREATNESS. They are at the core of it.**

Death is inevitable for every one of us. All the wealth and material resources we leave behind at some point in time will fade away. All other things will pass away. The only thing that will last is the seed/word of God, a measure of the Holy Spirit that we carry, share and transfer to others that will last. And those only come in a humble vessel and sold out life to Christ. This type of greatness is found in a heart totally surrendered to the master. This type of greatness even death cannot hold it captive. Jesus was basically telling them in Matthew 20 that to be truly great, your life must be a poured out offering. You cannot have your life kept selfish and lived for yourself and be truly great. True greatness has something to do with humility. "Humble yourselves therefore under the mighty hand of God, that he may exalt you in due time:" 1 Peter 5:6.

Like you, we want to be great also. But that quest has led us to a key findings in scripture. Jesus Christ not only shared this principle with us. He actually became the greatest by following this same principle he taught. His greatness was inherent in his humility and service - even to the point of death.

Only the meek will experience true greatness in the end; not the proud (Matthew 5:5). "Think of yourselves the way Christ Jesus thought of himself. He had equal status with God but didn't think so much of himself that he had to cling to the advantages of that status no matter what. Not at all. When the time came, he set aside the privileges of deity and took on the status of a slave, became human! Having become human, he stayed human. It was an incredibly humbling process. He didn't claim special privileges. Instead, he lived a selfless, obedient life and then died a selfless, obedient death—and the worst kind of death at that—a crucifixion" Philippians 2:5-8 (MSG).

Now, check out the result of service and humility. See how both led to greatness:
"Because of that obedience, God lifted him high and honored him far beyond anyone or anything, ever, so that all created beings in heaven and on earth—even those long ago dead and buried—will bow in worship before this Jesus Christ, and call out in praise that he is the Master of all, to the glorious honor of God the Father." (Philippians 2:9-11 MSG)

So it appears we have thought of greatness from a wrong perspective all these while. Wouldn't it make sense to trace true greatness to humility and service to God and to humanity? _ "So here's what I want you to do, God helping you: Take your everyday, ordinary life—your sleeping, eating, going-to-work, and walking-around life—and place it before God as an offering. Embracing what God does for you is the best thing you can do for him. Don't become so well-adjusted to your culture that you fit into it without even thinking. Instead, fix your attention on God. You'll be changed from the inside out. Readily recognize what he wants from you, and quickly respond to it. Unlike the culture around you, always dragging you down to its level of immaturity, God brings the best out of you, develops well-formed maturity in you." (Romans 12:1-2 MSG).

This type of greatness is wrapped in love for people – our friends. "There is no greater love than to lay down one's life for one's friends." (John 15:13). Unknown, hidden or disguisedly apparent to many, a heart of service is usually what naturally makes you want to help others solve their problem. And we have seen this element of service-greatness in some of the greatest discoveries in our time. Many of the ground breaking ideas that has helped humanity have their roots in a heart of service. A heart of service leads to problem solving. And problem solving leads to innovation and more creative ideas. Does that sound familiar to true entrepreneurs? Can you connect this to say the Facebook story for example? You will see a core service to humanity model at the centre of all that is being done. But we can take this further now that we have a better depth. **To solve the ultimate problem of live and the biggest puzzle of humanity, Christ, the seed of faith is the best we can ever give. The seed of the Holy Spirit – a measure of God – is the best we could ever give. This type of gift is transgenerational.**

Here's is another big one. The greatness we are longing for is not outside. It is inside. God made you and designed you great. As we surrender and reach for the depth of his power and grace; as we are being transformed inside-out from the common to the supernatural; as we advance in humility and grow in serving people (God's creation) we will be amazed at the way God transforms our lives for greatness (See Appendix 7 on operating from the core of God made you). God is simply saying to us today: "I have made you great. I have coded greatness into your DNA. You are born of me. Let me lead. Let me take charge. Let me use you to surprise the world with uncommon greatness. Allow me. Humble yourself before me. I will lift you up"

Your ordinary life is labeled greatness. You are born great. Because of what Christ has done you seize to be ordinary. You are an extraordinary being. Can I summon those who are working so hard and determined to be successful and great to take a look at it from this deeper perspective? It is our demonstration of love to humanity that is the greatness. A desire to give something that is of eternal value. Today, God is calling those of us who will offer up our lives as a sacrifice of love and service to a world that so desperately need it. In whatever profession or capacity we find ourselves, the path to greatness is always going to be the one that puts others first.

Reflection Points:

Not an easy road and I know this is quiet contrary to the "me first" ideology already ingrained in us. But we can turn a new leaf today by being determined to be a blessing, to give, to share, to love and sacrificially take up our responsibilities before God and men – going over and beyond the average and giving humanity the very best God has deposited in us. The best place to start is to first get this God. How can we give what we don't have? How do we love if we do not know God who is love Himself (1John 4:7-8)? How do we have true humility and a heart of service to humanity if we have not first been broken by God's word?

Personal Action and Development:

Where are those that truly want to be great? Can we start with humility-laden service and allow the mighty hand of God lift us up both here on earth and into eternity. Can we leave profound love in the hearts of men and in the sands of history. Today is another opportunity. There is only one life. The best way to keep it is to give it. The pathway to be great is to be poured out as an offering. So where do you want to start? From your home? Demonstrate greatness. At your place of work? Demonstrate greatness everywhere. Wherever you can, show love, serve with humility. Give something that will help others succeed both here on earth and beyond. We hope this book will inspire you to do that. We will see you on the path of true greatness :)

NO FEAR IN LOVE. TRUE LOVE TAKES AWAY FEAR AND REPLACES IT WITH FREEDOM. FREEDOM UNLEASHES ENERGY TO ENTER NEW FRONTIERS OF LEARNING AND GROWTH.

There is no fear in love; but perfect love casteth out fear: because fear hath torment. He that feareth is not made perfect in love (1 John 4: 18). Jesus said unto him, Thou shalt love the Lord thy God with all thy heart, and with all thy soul, and with all thy mind. And the second is like unto it, Thou shalt love thy neighbour as thyself (Matthew 22:37,39)

LOVE IS THE GREATEST - BECOME PART OF ITS REVOLUTION

The need for love is critical in our modern day. Everybody wants to be loved. Psychologists agree that one of our greatest need as human being is to love and be loved. No barrier can withstand the mighty force of love. Love is the greatest phenomenon in the world -- the greatest privilege and power known to man. Yet, in its most sincere and purest form, true love appears to be scarce today.

People cheating and hitting on each other. Hate crimes on the increase. Murder, war and rivalry are spiking. We begin to ask ourselves: where is Love? We found that those of us who profess it don't fully know its meaning or maybe we sometimes just forget about it and just live our lives. **Or how come that despite majority of the songs and hit tracks that sold millions and the popular ones we listen to today on radio and TV are Love-themed yet we witness the opposite in our society today?** Hate, slander, backbiting, etc. How can we explain such phenomenon? Are we just demonstrating superficial love that does not carry any weight or substance? Are we just carrying empty fluff in our hearts calling it love?

But love still beckons on us today: "I am worth fighting for." And that is why instead of answering about laws, rules, commands and external requirement, Jesus answered the commandment questions in Matthew 22:26-40 with "love responses" that addresses matters of the heart: Love God, Love your neighbours. It therefore means that instead of working extra hard to fulfill ALL other conditions and criteria to attain perfection, loving God first and then people around us is the two most important commandments for our whole life.

We see examples of this demonstration of true love with the quality of life of the first-century Christian. During this time the idea of love and self-sacrifice was foreign. Greeks, Romans, Gentiles, and Jews hated one another. But as they observed Christians from many nations, with different languages and cultures, actually loving one another and sacrificing to help each other, they responded in amazement, "Behold, how these people love one another!" (Report of Aristides, sent by the Emperor Hadrian to spy out those strange creatures known as "Christians." From the book *Hope Again: When Life Hurts and Dreams Fade* by Charles R. Swindoll). The early century Christians out of love "shared everything they had...There were no needy people among them, because those who owned land or houses would sell them and bring the money to give those in need" (Acts 4:32-37).

The ultimate love we want to present to you today is Agape Love, God's supernatural, unconditional love. This type of love is revealed supremely through Jesus Christ's death on the cross for our sins (John 3:16, John 15:13). It is the supernatural love He wants to produce in you and through you to others, by His Holy Spirit. Agape love is given because of the character of the person loving rather than because of the worthiness of the object of that love. Sometimes it is **love "in spite of"** rather than **"because of."** This is the love that liberates and sets free. Because of such great love that knows no height or depth or boundaries that we can arise in freedom and hope. This freedom gives us the energy to live, learn, grow and accomplish more in our lifetime.

If we lack this type of love yet speak in diverse tongues, have deep understanding, knowledge skills and competencies even to the point of doing outstanding things including giving to the needy, it will profit nothing. "If I speak in the tongues of men or of angels, but do not have love, I am only a resounding gong or a clanging cymbal." 1 Corinthians 13:1 (NIV). It literally means I am just full of fluff, making empty noise, without any practical relevance, if I don't love genuinely as God loves.

This book is written from an individual and organization perspective. While individuals would have easily connected with our narratives in this section on love, we don't want it to elude corporations and institutions too. As we mentioned in a related section in this book, we are seeing more and more that it is unbusinesslike qualities such as love for our co-workers, employees and the community of consumers we serve that sets us apart as a superior brand. We don't want to delve too much into the aspect of free market capitalism versus corporate social responsibility models of business enterprises as it will elude the scope of this book. But this one thing is our desire, that your heart would be tuned to something deeper than money and profit.

For those of us who have found love, let's cherish it, nurture it and allow it to grow as it liberates us and others around us. True love forgives other's wrong doing and sees past "in spite of" their faults. No matter what perspective life has turned to you, we can still choose agape love - unconditional. Let's take our love life to a higher level. Let's love our spouses, children, community, people, our pets, everyone around us with true love. For those who are still on the earnest search for true love, don't give up yet. Keep searching because true love is out there.

As I got to this juncture in my journey of life that I realize that it's more than just words. It's more than just saying "I love you." I have to become an instrument of love in my time. I have concluded in my heart that one of the strongest way I can demonstrate my love is to encourage, inspire and motivate other people around me. I found encouragement to be a powerful gesture. It is lifting other peoples' hands up. I know I can't do much in most cases but through my words of encouragements and in certain situations where I practically encourage the hands and efforts of others, I am demonstrating love. Recently, I took my love life to social media. A funny thing I started doing anytime I am on social media (Facebook) is to "love" people's post instead of just liking it. I read and make the concerted effort to "love." I see Facebook "likes" to be cheap, just a click. But love requires pressing and holding until the love button pops up. If you have additional time, say a few words of encouragement. It means a lot especially in today's virtual reality world where someone needs that encouragement. We can do this for each other. We can create an environment where love prevails over hate and where we empower and strengthen each other to greatness.

As a family, we adopted 1 John 4: 18 as our guiding scripture. We have seen love liberate and consequentially generate energy that have allowed us to experience growth and progress. This book is a product of love and we pray that as you have read it, you become liberated too. We encourage you to join us in this love revolution today and let's make the world a better place.

Reflection Points:
Let's be honest, true love takes work. But the results of loving genuinely as God loves is remarkable. We can see people genuinely change when they come in contact with a solidly grounded love. So we put it to you do you love God, yourself and people around you as God loves? Whether yes or no, we can all do better starting today. Let's take it a notch higher. Show some love.

Personal Action and Development:
Show some love to people around you. Like we have recommended in this book, ensure it is sustainable and not just out of a sudden excitement. Ground your

understanding on the fact that if God can love you as a person despite your faults and inadequacies then you should love too. Remember, this is a command. So list out ten people who you feel need love within your circle today and impress upon them that you love them with God's kind of love – Agape love. You may want to add people that offended you before to forgive and love them **despite** their shortcomings. This is how we change the world with the power of love. Welcome to the revolutions. Please find further study and conversation on Love at www.oyeseducation.org/resources.

EXCEPT YOU LIVED IN THE 1967 JAMES BOND FILM TITLED "YOU ONLY LIVE TWICE", YOU ONLY GET ONE CHANCE TO LIVE. IF LIVED WISELY AND RIGHTLY, THAT ONCE IS ENOUGH TO CREATE A LASTING IMPACT.

"Teach us to realize the brevity of life, so that we may grow in wisdom." (Psalm 90:12 NLT). "And as it is appointed unto men once to die, but after this the judgment". (Hebrews 9:27)

ONLY ONE LIFE

There is no duplicate for life. It is not a James Bond film, it is reality. Life is in session and prudence demands that we learn to "number our days, that we may gain a heart of wisdom" Psalm 90:12 (NIV). What does it mean to number our days? It's not the ability to count how many days we have lived or to predict how many days we have left. Numbering our days mean, as the NLT Bible puts it, realizing the "brevity of life." It means knowing that we only have so many days on this earth, and therefore we want to "seize the day," living each day to the fullest.

With this one life, we can change the course of history. With the single opportunity we have, we can leave lasting legacies that will make life better for those coming behind us. It's not waiting till New Year's resolution time. It is waking up today and maximizing the power of each day. It is getting a clear vision for our lives and walking in our unique life path. It is living intentionally and determinedly in line with our God given purposes as divine originals. It is making every second, minute and hour count. It is taking responsibility for our growth and not waiting on chance for personal development to happen. It is going through the change process, shifting gears and being around people that encourages us to grow. It is leaving our comfort zone and solving problems, adding value to ourselves and investing in the lives of others.

Research has shown that we have about 80,000hours of worktime in our lifetime. When we recognize that we have only so much time on this earth, that truth will help us think rightly about how to spend our time (see Appendix 6 for a life timeline illustration). Understanding this, in turn, will encourage us to grow in wisdom. We will want to judge well how to use the time allotted to us, and this requires godly perspective. It's not

157

just knowing what we can do, but also what we should do. When we number our days, we will strive to fill each one with value, living every moment for God's purposes and glory.

My elder brother once made a profound statement that I will never forget. This was his advice: "it is better to invest in 'life stock' (people) than to invest in the stock market" Over the years, no other statement is as true to me as this. Investing in people although may not yield immediate material or financial reward, but knowing that they will in turn become better off and ultimately lead good lives is a collective win for every one of us. **Future generation will benefit from a life that was positively impacted beyond financial reward.**

Today, I am reminded of what I came across in Harvard Business Review *10 Must Reads on Managing Yourself* (2010, page 8): "People who are driven to excel have this unconscious propensity to underinvest in their families and over invest in their careers – even though intimate and loving relationships with their families are the most powerful and enduring source of happiness". Another very renowned research institute asked top CEOs and Senior Management officials of highly successful companies what they regretted the most after they retired. About 72.5% of them identified that they regretted not spending time with their families and in particular their children. Make your life count as an investment to people around you. It will be worth it in the end. **The journey starts today, right now. The clock is ticking. You have only one life, how would you live it?**

Solomon writes: 'Seize life! Eat bread with gusto … Oh, yes - God takes pleasure in your pleasure! Dress festively every morning. Don't skimp on colours and scarves. Relish life with the spouse you love … every day of your precarious life. Each day is God's gift. It's all you get in exchange for the hard work of staying alive. Make the most of each one! Whatever turns up, grab it and do it. And heartily! This is your last and only chance ... for there's neither work to do nor thoughts to think in the company of the dead, where you're most certainly headed' (Ecclesiastes 9: 7-10 MSG). So, what are you waiting for? To graduate? To get married? To have children? To retire? **Life is about the journey, not just the destination!** Your life is here and now, your family is here and now, your marriage is here and now, your career is here and now. The journey takes place every day, and you can find meaning when you search for a greater purpose. You can find small joys every day if you have eyes of faith.

Solomon recognized that ultimately we all end up at the same destination - the grave. The only difference lies in how much we enjoy the journey. **Instead of obsessing over the things you can't control, focus on what you can control and leave the rest to God. You've got only one life!**

Reflection Points:

On a normal day, how would you say you applied wisdom and lived purposefully? Do you feel challenged to live more purposefully daily? On occasions when you feel fulfilled what did you do or didn't do? Are there regular activities in your life that you would eliminate from your schedule if you were to number your days wisely? Are there new ones you would like to add? Do you agree with us that it is daily small adjustments that lead to bigger results in the end?

Personal Action and Development:

Go over your life plan again. Start by reviewing your daily, weekly and monthly routine. Don't wait till New Year's Day. Do it today. Carefully evaluate people you are spending time with, the places you spend most time at, how you spend your money, the investment you are making in the lives of others and so on. Do you see a need to make adjustments? List a few things you intend to do better on and pray to God about it. We will be happy to know about your progress. Only one life; make the most of it.

◻

PERSONAL NOTE AND CREATIVE SPACE

PERSONAL NOTE AND CREATIVE SPACE

PERSONAL NOTE AND CREATIVE SPACE

POST-SCRIPT

Whether you purchased this book or it was given to you as a gift, we want to thank you for taking the time to read through. We have no doubt in our hearts that you have been challenged and blessed at the same time.

As you would have already observed, this book is based on Biblical foundations. To us, spiritual values take precedence. We are keen on this because we believe God is the source of all creation. We also believe that every person was created to fulfill a divine purpose and that the Bible holds the ultimate principle to help individuals accomplish their God-given purpose. While many separate what they believe from business and other aspects of their lives, ours is inseparable. God is at the centre of everything we do. And what we profess is not religion, it is a way of life. If we had the opportunity of adding one more quote to this book, it would be the one below:

CHRISTIANITY IS MORE THAN MERE RELIGION. IT GOES MORE THAN JUST BEING BORN AGAIN, IT IS A LIFESTYLE. IT IS A CULTURE OF BEING A NEW CREATURE AND KNOWING THAT THE HOLY SPIRIT DWELLS WITHIN.

We hope that by providing side by side Biblical context in our narratives and discussion in this book, we have been able to challenge you to a standard that is higher, greater and unchanging. We hope the Christian businessman is encouraged towards excellence even as those who are intending to ensure that their businesses align with Biblical principles find this as a guide book. We pray that you will find a reason to LIVE a life of purpose, LOVE God, yourself and others sincerely, LEARN from every situation no matter what and GROW to the fullness of your potential in life.

We are fully aware that several of the sections require further work. Please bear with us in this first publication.

Pray along with us as we work on expounding and expanding the ideas through discussions and other talking points. Your support and encouragement will go a long way in helping reach more people with a new paradigm for appropriating values our lives and in running our business in contemporary times.

For those who don't yet believe, we invite you to Jesus Christ not because we want you to become religious. But because we want you to live the rest of your life in purpose. Throughout history and up till today, there has been many effort to appease God and to find the ultimate truth in life. It is human to keep learning and yet not come to the knowledge of the truth (2 Timothy 3:7; 1 Cor. 2:14). The issue of sin and carnality is constantly wrestling within. Our carnal nature is constantly wrestling with the truth and righteousness. But the truth is standard, we cannot do anything against the truth (2Corinthians 13:8). And God's word is that truth that can save (John 17:17). "And you shall know the truth, and the truth shall make you free" (John 8:32). So we invite you to partake in the truth.

Doing good deeds, meditating on whatever we so choose, being kind and nice and so on cannot save. Salvation is in only one, Christ Jesus, in whose name everyone who believe will be saved (Acts 4:12). Access the fullness of who you are today. Discover the truth about your existence that you were loved and created by a loving God. Receive the free gift of salvation (Ephesians 2:8-9). You will be amazed at how accepting this truth into your heart will cause you to live purposefully, love genuinely and learn through every situation until you grow into the very image of Christ Jesus. We welcome you to the family of those of us striving to appropriate godly values, as light and salts (Matthew 5:13-16), in our everyday, ordinary lives.

Now that you made the choice to become a Christian, make effort to read the Bible because this is how you will grow. It may not be an easy thing to do if you are a

165

new Christian and not of the habit but reading five minutes a day can help you to start off. Here are a few scriptures to get you started:

Psalm 32:3-7
Proverbs 3:5-8
Psalm 139:14
2 Timothy 2:21-22
Romans 8:16
John 14: 15
Matthew 5:43-48

The book of John is another great place to start in discovering more about who God is and what He promises to those who believe in Him. Proverbs is another good place to start reading. It provides sound bites of wisdom for everyday matters that we face as individuals. Read Bible passages slowly and attentively a couple times and if you find unfamiliar words or ideas, feel free to ask older, mature and Bible believing Christians or pastors who you can trust to help you understand what you're reading. Personalize it and focus on a word or phrase that speaks to you on a personal level. Pray that the Holy Spirit will make God's Word clear to you. Keep reflecting and meditating on the Word of God, the Bible.

We will be more than happy to celebrate with those who are just making this step. Whether you are young, old, a business man, professional of any sort and you now accept this truth we are talking about, we celebrate you! There's no age difference here. We are all members of the family of God. We are all one in Christ. Let's continue the conversation. We will be more than happy to hear from you through the LIVE LOVE LEARN GROW community across various channels. Let us raise the banner and lead higher. Great things can still happen in our life time. Believe.

Blessings!

Appendices
Appendix 1: The Value Adding Loop

The Value Adding Framework for individuals, teams and leaders

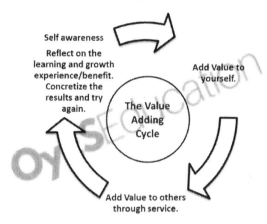

Self awareness

Reflect on the learning and growth experience/benefit. Concretize the results and try again.

Add Value to yourself.

The Value Adding Cycle

Add Value to others through service.

*1: ADD VALUE TO YOURSELF. Be taught. Be fed. Be trained. Be equipped. You have to first be transformed before you can become an agent of transformation in your generation. Read books. Listen to great teachers. Ask intelligent questions and take note of when they are been answered. You need to develop a sustainable source and fine tune the process of being refilled. Have a VALUABLE source. The fundamental, prima facia and most important value add is Jesus Christ. This is key because believe in Christ releases the seed of God (and greatness), the Holy Spirit, into your life. This will totally transform how you see and what I see. You will be able to see beyond the mundane into the supernatural. You will have access to the most VALUEBLE source and not just the available resources. The truth, the Word of God became real as virtue is deposited inside of you. Virtues are like springs or wells that never run dry.

2: ADD VALUE TO OTHERS THROUGH SERVICE AND PROBLEM SOLVING. As you have received the grace and abilities, begin to take action. Don't just sit on it. But it's important to take note of where people miss it at this point. Where most people miss it is when they start out thinking that money is the ward for the value (virtue) they carry so as a result they serve or share less. The result of that is continuous erosion and depreciation of your value. The reason is because in this value adding framework, the way to sustain in is to keep have a heart that wants to keep learning more. It is an EXPERIENTIAL LEARNING PROCESS; learning by doing. Over time, you will be valued and appreciated for your worth. Your worth or compensation will be commensurate to the problems you solve. Sometimes, even money cannot capture the worth or compensation. Continue to be a blessing. Serve. Help others. Encourage people everywhere.

3: SELF EVALUATION/AWARENESS. This is probably the most important component and the easily missed out. Reflect on the learning and growth experience/benefit. Concretize the results. Good or bad, success or failure, hard or easy, whatever it is, there is something to learn from it. That is your portion. That is the VALUABLE piece to carry on to the next phase. Be patient with yourself. Understand that even when you attempt to add value to others sometimes, the outcomes are negative. Don't feel too bad or beat yourself down. Remember, it's a loop. Reflect on what you learnt and make it a profit instead of a loss. The learning experience will most usually become an asset (which leads to the next phase in the loop). Most times it's usually our own approach or an issue of timing. Don't let anything kill your enthusiasm. Keep doing what God has laid in your heart. Do what you know you are born to do. Live to the height of your calling.

Please visit www.oyeseducation.org/resources to access the full explanation of the value adding loop including a video where we showed its application in real life situations.

Appendix 2: Becoming a better version of yourself by adding value to yourself. This is an extension of the Value adding Loop.

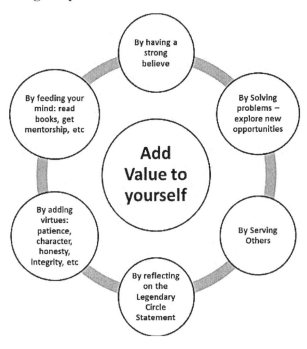

Appendix 3: The Power of Solitude shows an analogical chemical fractional distillation process compared to a mind filled with many mixtures of stuff but needs to be clarified into pure thoughts or ideas.

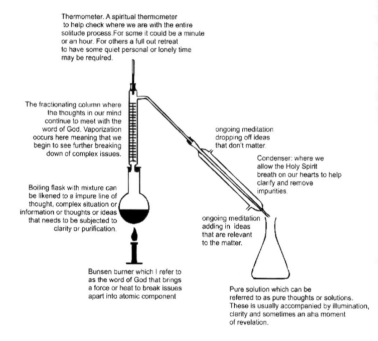

Thermometer. A spiritual thermometer to help check where we are with the entire solitude process. For some it could be a minute or an hour. For others a full out retreat to have some quiet personal or lonely time may be required.

The fractionating column where the thoughts in our mind continue to meet with the word of God. Vaporization occurs here meaning that we begin to see further breaking down of complex issues.

ongoing meditation dropping off ideas that don't matter.

Condenser: where we allow the Holy Spirit breath on our hearts to help clarify and remove impurities.

Boiling flask with mixture can be likened to a impure line of thought, complex situation or information or thoughts or ideas that needs to be subjected to clarity or purification.

ongoing meditation adding in ideas that are relevant to the matter.

Bunsen burner which I refer to as the word of God that brings a force or heat to break issues apart into atomic component

Pure solution which can be referred to as pure thoughts or solutions. These is usually accompanied by illumination, clarity and sometimes an aha moment of revelation.

Appendix 4: Legendary Relationship/Circle Tenet/Statement

"In my relationship(s):

I want to constantly be challenged to get better. We are vision oriented. Integrity is our watchword. Our focus should be forward-looking. The atmosphere we create must be affirming and encouraging. We desire to often be out of our comfort zones and explore the learning zone. We want to meet each other with excitement. Failure is not our enemy, we see it as part of the process. We are willing to have meaningful, sincere yet sometimes hard conversations. We all win together. We are all growing and advancing. We desire change for the better. Continuous growth is modeled and expected."

This tenet was inspired by John C. Maxwell's *15 Invaluable Laws of Growth*

Appendix 5: Comfort Zone versus Learning Zone (Growth Zone) versus Panic Zone (Breaking Point)

Comfort Zone versus Learning Zone (Growth Zone) versus Breaking Point

The concept of marginality applies here. We only focus on BIG changes. Aiming for a BIG change can be overwhelming sometimes and even lead to breaking points. A good way to go is to take one step at a time and make it sustainable. Small incremental changes can lead to great gain over time

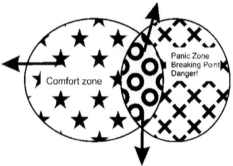

Learning Zone
Stretch Zone
Change Occurs Here

80% of people live here. They don't want to be challenge or disturbed.

common victims of this zone are high achievers and successful people who feel there is nothing more to achieve. Success can be a limiting factor and a precursor for staying in a comfort zone.

Panic Zone
Breaking Point
Danger!

Comfort zone

Growth Zone

- Great things never come from comfort zone
- Life begins at the end of your comfort zone. Break loose from your inertia!

Appendix 6: Only One life: Make the most of your lucrative time while you are alive – especially the 20s

The 20s is an extremely important part of our lives. Part of who I am today and my Biblical foundations were formed at this stage. I have come to form the impression that it is the most vital time in any human life yet the part that could end up being most wasted if we fail to apply wisdom. Clinical psychologist Meg Jay alludes to how critical the 20s can be in her 2013 TED talk titled "Why 30 is not the new 20"

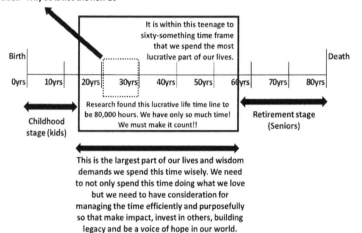

Please watch the TED talk by Meg Jay titled: *Why 30 is not the new 20*. Also visit www.80000hours.org for more info on how you can make the right career choices, help solve the world's most pressing problems, as well as have a more rewarding, interesting life.

"...I write to you, young men, because you are strong, and the word of God lives in you, and you have overcome the evil one." 1 John 2:14c

"Teach us to realize the brevity of life, so that we may grow in wisdom." (Psalm 90:12 NLT).

Appendix 7: Operating from within, knowing who you are in Christ at the core and living out your godly identity in a world with many false alternatives.

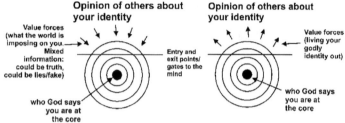

How do you define who you are (Your Identity):

A Responses:
1. Based on what you have i.e. the money or material thing
2. Based on what you do i.e. career or job
3. What other people say about you i.e. brother, sister, sinner

B Responses:
Defining yourself based on godly criteria as the chosen of God; unique and original
1. You are blessed: gifted beyond measure
2. You are broken: embracing your brokeness strengthens your spiritual awakening and thirst
3. You are given: As an offering to serve with humility, to bless, to restore and revive. you are given as a divine original, a masterpiece to solve a specific problem as you operate from within.

the reality of many of us as we continue in a state ongoing conflict between what the world is saying we are and who we know we are in Christ. The place of solitude helps us clarify our thoughts as the word of God permeates our atmosphere.

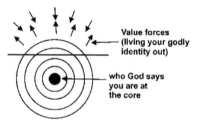

More linking points on this:

*"If you don't stand for something you will inadvertently fall for anything."

*"Divine Originals"
*Your identity in Christ
*"Mindset"
*Created for a purpose.
*Don't copy or compete
*God is at work in you

ABOUT THE AUTHORS

Oluwaseun and Channon Oyeniran met in Hull, UK in 2010 during their Masters studies and three years later, in 2013 got married and are currently settled in Canada. They are a typical modern day family with strong Christian values. Both in their early 30s, they believe their family is set up divinely as an answer to the call of this generation in propagating and spreading empirical Biblical truth. They are actively involved in the community and could be found either playing sports or spending time encouraging and inspiring people, especially youths.

Their passion and desire is to help individuals and families grow in the areas of sustainable personal development, relationships (vertical with God and horizontal with people including marital), Christianity in a multicultural society, leadership, fatherhood and motherhood among other areas. They both work full time in the City of Toronto and are also founders of Oyeniran Education Support Services (OyES) which is an out-of-classroom modern day teaching and learning platform built on Biblical principles and created to minister to people across the globe.

They live in Ontario, Canada with their lovely son and are more than happy to speak at your events on any of the topics discussed in this book as well as to inspire and encourage. You can reach out to them if you want to have further conversations on the themes and topics discussed in this book or if you just want to have a random chat with them. You can reach them through phone (647-785-6798) or email (contact@oyeseducation.org).

DO YOU KNOW THAT ALL OF THE OPENING QUOTES IN THIS BOOK ARE ORIGINAL AND ARE AVAILABLE IN PICTURE FRAMES? AND DO YOU ALSO KNOW THAT THIS BOOK COMES WITH EVEN MORE ACCOMPANYING RESOURCES TO HELP YOU ENGAGE CULTURE?

Each quote in this book have some level of depth so we went further to carefully craft each quote into 8.5" X 8.5" picture frames. Kindly visit the dedicated book store: www.oyeseducation.org to order one or more. Place them on the walls, book shelves, study rooms or office tables to create positive vibes for everyday living.

Even more, visit the website for PostCard sizes of each quote as well as a T-Shirt to carry on the message. These are accompanying resources that you will love so make sure to join the movement of those who are living, loving, learning and growing.

THIS BOOK IS ALSO AVAILABLE IN E-BOOK FORMAT ON AMAZON KINDLE.

WATCHOUT FOR THE COFFEE TABLE EDITION OF THIS BOOK – A COLOURFUL EDITION WITH OUSTANDING GRAPHICS AND LAYOUT. THE COFFEE TABLE EDITION WILL FIT PUBLIC SPACES PERFECTLY AND HELP YOU TO ENGAGE IN MEANINGFUL POSITIVE CONVERSATIONS THAT WILL RESULT IN GROWTH.

Follow the book

f   @LiveLoveLearnGrowBook

⊙   @LiveLoveLearnGr

⊙   @LiveLoveLearnGrow_

Social media hashtags for this book:
#LiveLoveLearnGrow #3LG

Follow the author

@seunoyeniran

Please follow me on social media (Facebook, Twitter, Instagram):

www.oyeseducation.org

Made in the USA
Middletown, DE
30 January 2018